Now you can enjoy the
homemade goodness of breads
of all kinds—without the fuss
of old-fashioned baking.

THE BREAD MACHINE COOKBOOK

*brings you tempting recipes for use with
your bread machine—including*

- Luscious White Bread
- Mixed-Grain Breads
- Sourdough Breads
- Whole-Wheat Pizza Dough
- Savory Breads
- Fruit Breads
- Vegetable Breads

. . . and much more!

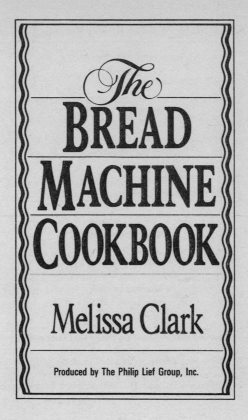

The
BREAD
MACHINE
COOKBOOK

Melissa Clark

Produced by The Philip Lief Group, Inc.

BERKLEY BOOKS, NEW YORK

THE BREAD MACHINE COOKBOOK

A Berkley Book / published by arrangement with
The Philip Lief Group, Inc.

PRINTING HISTORY
Berkley edition / May 1993

ISBN: 0-425-13733-3

A BERKLEY BOOK ® TM 757,375
Berkley Books are published by The Berkley Publishing Group,
200 Madison Avenue, New York, New York 10016.
The name "BERKLEY" and the "B" logo
are trademarks belonging to Berkley Publishing Corporation.

PRINTED IN THE UNITED STATES OF AMERICA

20 19 18 17 16 15 14 13 12 11

THIS BOOK IS DEDICATED TO MY FATHER,
WHO WILL ALWAYS BE MY MENTOR
BREAD BAKER.

Acknowledgments

I would like to express gratitude to the many people who were so giving with their time and energy during the writing of this book. Foremost, there is the Regal Corporation, and Zojirushi, who so generously donated bread machines for me to test these recipes with. Then, there are the people who helped and encouraged me along the way: Amy Martin, who painstakingly proofread the entire manuscript; Julia Banks, my editor, for her unlimited patience and guidance; and Molly Logan and Max Jonson who helped me eat all that bread.

CONTENTS

INTRODUCTION

I grew up in a home where freshly baked bread was the standard, and all the flaccid, presliced loaves sold in the supermarket fell into the same category of food as Twinkies and potato chips. The yeasty scent of any bakery takes me back to my childhood kitchen, where my father kneaded walnuts and chopped onions into smooth, tan dough. Under his strong hands, the gummy mass became dull and springy, and when I would try to pull off a knob to eat raw, the dough sprang back at me as if in protest.

Bread baking was a Saturday ritual, and took my father most of the day. Rising bowls of dough were carefully wrapped with plastic and blanketed in towels while I was admonished not to open the backdoor lest a draft knock down the bread that was struggling to "double in bulk." The dough was vigorously kneaded at least once more, shaped into loaves, and allowed to rise again. Finally, while it was baking, my father would spray water and throw ice cubes into the oven to make the steam essential for a crispy crust. At the end of this long afternoon, the kitchen sink was full of dried yeast-covered measuring cups and spoons, flour and water paste encrusted the countertops, and gluey drips of molasses splattered the floor and were tracked all over the house. The cleanup was no fun.

But eating the finished loaf was. Dense, rich, and chewy crusts surrounded nutty, soft centers, and the family debated fiercely over whether the outside or the inside of the bread was better. We never could decide because it was all so good.

Once on my own as a professional caterer, I tried to follow my father's example and dazzle my clients with homemade bread. I worked hard to keep my Saturdays free, but bread baking was too tyrannical. I soon chose freedom—and bought my bread from a very good bakery. While the loaves were tasty and well textured, only the most expensive came near the bread my father baked, and this was impractical for purchasing in the quantity necessary for a large party. Besides, I missed the aroma from the kitchen wafting throughout the house. That first warm slice on which butter would melt into yellow pools.

So I was jubilant when asked to write a book on bread machines. Finally a way to improve myself professionally and provide customers with homemade bread. I have to admit that when bread machines first came out, I was very snobbish about them. I did not believe that real bread could come from a computerized box; it would certainly not meet the standards of the many bread-loving party throwers who employ me. Hundreds of loaves later, I feel ridiculous for my past prejudices. Although the bread machine cannot (nor does it attempt to) do everything a human bread baker can, what it can do it does excellently and painlessly—a flawless combination.

Now I can whip out several impressive, uniform loaves *while I do other things*. This is the beauty of it. No baby-sitting, punching down, shaping, and tapping—just pressing a button. And savoring the aroma of hot bread, which is strong enough to make my neighbors unconsciously smile in the corridors. Ripping apart that warm loaf with my bare hands to watch the steam rise from the crumb. Controlling what goes into my bread. Setting marmalade bread on the timer, and waking up to a feast.

Of course, the bread machine cannot do some kinds of bread, like crispy French baguettes or focaccia, without my assistance. But it does cut my labor in half. I can put in the ingredients, turn the machine on its dough setting, and come back an hour and a half later to shape and bake. Or I can make the dough, refrigerate it, and shape and bake it later when I have time to sit around and wait on a second rising. For very little work on my part, the results are truly miraculous.

BRIEF HISTORY OF BREAD BAKING

Bread, in some form, has been linked with civilization for thousands of years. In the all-out history of humans, this is not as long as we think, and for centuries before raised loaves were developed, gruel was the staple in people's diet. Gruel is essentially any grain that is cooked down with water until it softens. The type of grain used was of course dictated by what was able to grow in the area; rice gruel was eaten in Asia, corn gruel in the Americas, and wheat gruel in Northern Africa and Europe.

Flat, unleavened cakes were inevitably the next step after gruel—when someone figured out that if gruel is left to dry out over heat, it becomes a hard, flat cake. Charred remains of flat grain cakes (made, incidentally, from the whole grain) were found in a prehistoric evacuation site in Western Europe. These cakes were probably eaten all over the world, and still are, in the delicious forms of tortillas in South and Central America, and pancakes in Asia.

The leap from flat cakes to bread was a bit more complicated, and has been credited to both the Hebrews and ancient Egyptians. We do know that leavened bread was around since the golden age of Egypt, as many paintings from that period depict scenes of the bread-baking process, from harvesting the wheat, to grinding and separating the grain, to eating the finished loaves. We know leavened bread was familiar to the Hebrews because the Old Testament prohibits its consumption during Passover, which meant it was common food for the rest of the year. Most likely, raised loaves were developed in several wheat-growing cultures around the same time: about 4000 B.C.

Wheat is the principal grain used in raised loaves because it is the only one containing enough gluten, the protein that traps the gas from the yeast and makes the dough rise. The first loaves were accidental, as yeast floating in the atmosphere settled in the dough for unleavened cakes, and fermented. The gases got trapped in the skinny, flat dough and made it grow fat. New loaves were made by saving a bit of the dough from old loaves, which were infested with the necessary yeast.

The ancient Greeks dramatically improved and refined bread baking. They developed mills that could grind the flour into different degrees of fineness. Flavorings, such as fruit, seeds, nuts, and spices, were added and dough variations were made with honey, milk, oil, eggs, and other liquids. It is said that there were over 160 varieties of bread made in Athens during this period.

In imperial Rome bread was baked at home in the rural areas, and by bakers in the cities. Pure wheaten bread was the most expensive and elite variety, and the whiter the flour, the more money it commanded. Most of the population, however, ate bread made from part wheat or rye (which also has a bit of gluten) and part barley or oats. It was a coarse, dark, heavy loaf, but sustaining nonetheless.

During the Middle Ages, bakers' guilds were formed in the cities, and bread baking was highly regulated. Short weighing was especially common, and London bakers began the practice of adding an extra bun for every dozen to avoid being dragged through the streets if charged with this offense. Hence the term "baker's dozen."

Thick slices of heavy bread known as "trenchers," sometimes colored yellow, blue, and pink for regal affairs, were used in the wealthiest households as a plate for highly sauced medieval meals. The sauce-soaked trenchers were usually given to the poor after the meat was eaten by the rich.

With the agricultural and technical advances of the upcoming centuries and the scientific revolution, softer, whiter bread became available to more of the population. Only over the past one hundred years, in a movement begun by Dr. Sylvester Graham, has whole-grain bread been thought to be healthier, although most of the population still prefers the whiter variety.

Today, bread baking has come a long way. The bread machine enables home bakers to make whatever kind of bread they choose, be it brown or white, with the flip of a switch. Yeast is stabilized and sold in little foil pouches, and an abundance of other ingredients is easily available. The one thing that has really remained the same over all these millenia is that we all still crave good bread. And we probably always will.

INGREDIENTS: KEEP IT SIMPLE

Since bread, in its most basic form, is made up of very few ingredients—flour, water, yeast, sugar, and usually shortening —the quality of these ingredients is paramount for achieving good flavor. While some of the recipes in this book and others may have ingredient lists that reach the bottom of the page, as with most good things, it is the quality of the ingredients rather than their quantity that counts. Take out the expensive sun-dried tomatoes packed in virgin olive oil, the exotic herbs and spices, fruit and nuts, and you are left with the three bread basics: flour, water, and leavening. And although all those additions can make for some very nice bread, if the unadulterated loaf was made with poor flour, the result will tell all. This means that you should buy stone-ground flour from sources you can trust. Health-food stores are generally, although not always, reliable for this. If you cannot find a good source for flour and grains near you, order them from one of the sources listed on page 198. Water should be the kind you would want to drink, which means tap water is fine for me in New York City. However, if you live in an area where the water is hard with minerals or is metallic, it is better to use bottled spring water, or to affix a filter to your kitchen sink. Table salt is fine for bread, although sea salt is saltier and better. Use the finest ingredients you can get, and each flaky slice will reward your effort.

FLOURS AND GRAINS

Since flour is the main ingredient in any bread, the type of flour used can greatly affect the outcome. Breads made with only white wheat flour will be lighter and rise higher than a bread made with whole-grain flours; however, whole-grain flours make for a lovely mealy texture. Buckwheat flour adds nuttiness, and soy flour has a slightly vegetable taste. Once you understand the characteristics of each flour, you will be able to achieve a myriad of flavors and textures by simply varying their proportions.

White Wheat Flour
Most bread, even that called "whole grain," is made up in part of white flour (three cups white flour and three cups whole wheat flour, for example). White flour has a fair amount of gluten, which, when mixed together with the yeast and liquid, creates the bread's skeleton. When the dough is kneaded, strands of gluten are woven into a web that traps the carbon dioxide gas given off by the yeast. The longer the bread is

kneaded (that tiresome exercise which you and I, as proud owners of bread machines, need no longer practice), the more gluten cells are intertwined, allowing them to collect enough carbon dioxide to expand. This expansion is what ultimately causes that initial hard lump of dough to rise and lighten.

Only flour made from wheat, and minimally from rye, has gluten, and therefore is the only type that will rise from yeast. White flour has a significantly higher proportion of gluten than whole-wheat flour. Each individual grain of wheat is made up of three layers: the bran that covers the outside, the endosperm that contains the gluten, and the germ in which the nutrients and oils are found. One of the biggest reasons the germ is almost always weeded out of flour is that the oils go rancid quickly, thereby lowering the shelf life. During the milling process, these layers are separated, and only the endosperm is ground for white flour (which, in its nascent form, is yellowish). As Harold McGee notes in his fascinating book *On Food and Cooking,* the word "flour" comes from the medieval notion of "flower," meaning the best of something, in this case, the endosperm. Therefore the term "whole-wheat flour," with the bran and germ included, would have been an oxymoron to a fifteenth-century baker, and even today whole wheat flour is called "wheatmeal" in England.

There are two common varieties of wheat made into white flour: hard and soft. Hard wheat flour (sold as bread flour) will form a stronger gluten network, and is therefore perfect for bread. Flour made from soft wheat (used in cake flour) has a fragile gluten structure, which, while not well suited for bread, produces the tender, flaky crumb of cakes and pastry.

All-purpose flour is the one you will most commonly see on supermarket shelves. It is a combination of both hard and soft wheat and is acceptable, but not great, for all kinds of home baking. Bleached flour has been whitened with unharmful chemicals, while unbleached flour has been allowed to whiten naturally (which happens when it is exposed to air for several weeks). Unbleached flour will produce a slightly better loaf because the airing process also serves to strengthen the gluten.

Bread flour is the flour of choice for this book. Use it as directed, and you will not be disappointed with your loaves. Don't even attempt to use all-purpose flour in a bread machine; the results are nearly inedible.

Whole-Wheat Flour

Whole-wheat flour contains particles from the whole grain of the wheat including the bran and germ. In most commercial whole-wheat flours, the bran and germ are first separated from the endosperm as if for white flour, and are later recombined. In stone-ground whole-wheat flour, the grains are never separated in the first place, and the texture is a bit coarser than that of regular whole wheat. As I mentioned above, in keeping faithful to the origin of the word ''flour,'' which once meant only white flour, the British call whole-wheat flour ''wheatmeal.''

The bran in whole-wheat flour gives the finished bread a deep color and a somewhat crunchy, earthy bite. It is a good source of fiber necessary for a balanced diet. The wheat germ adds many important nutrients such as vitamin B and E, and iron.

Loaves made from only whole-wheat flour are heavy and tightly packed because the gluten content of whole-wheat flour is lower than that of white flour. Not only is the amount of endosperm less per measure in whole-wheat flour compared with white flour, but during kneading, the sharp bits of bran and germ can rupture what few gluten strands exist. While some people prefer the density of such loaves, others mix their whole-wheat flour with bread flour, add more yeast, or boost the gluten content with a few tablespoons of straight gluten flour. In this book, for the most part I have used a combination of bread and whole-wheat flours to achieve chewy, not-too-heavy loaves.

Semolina Flour

Generally used for pasta, this flour is not widely found in breads outside of Italy and Greece, although it makes for a very nice loaf. Made from hard wheat flour, semolina is ground from the endosperm in larger chunks than regular bread flour, resulting in a supremely stable structure. This is the hardest wheat flour you can buy, and makes for exceptionally well-risen loaves with a nutty flavor and a pale yellow interior.

Gluten Flour

Gluten flour is the pure protein removed from the endosperm of wheat grains. The starch is rinsed off, and the protein is then processed into flour. Since it is the gluten in wheat flour that makes the dough rise, pure gluten can easily be added to whole-grain breads to lighten their normally dense texture. Gluten can also be used alone to produce a starch-free bread, but the texture is rather flabby. I use gluten in small quantities in addition to other grains for a nicely risen, whole-meal bread.

Graham Flour
Developed by Dr. Sylvester Graham at the beginning of the nineteenth century, this flour is composed of very finely milled whole wheat. It is good to use in bread in addition to its more common use in crackers of the same name. Graham flour produces a lighter loaf than regular whole wheat, because the bran is ground more finely and is therefore less likely to pierce the gluten cells.

Wheat Bran
The bran is the outer covering of any grain, in this case of wheat. It is generally sifted out of flour during the milling process, but is later added back into whole-wheat flour. Bran has a bit of protein, vitamins, and minerals, but it is best known for its prodigious quantity of fiber, which, as we've all been told, is necessary to a well-balanced diet and healthy intestines. You will sometimes see wheat bran sold in boxes as ''miller's bran''; it is exactly the same.

Wheat Germ
Wheat germ refers to the innermost part of the wheat berry, which contains the embryo of the new plant. It is an extremely nutrient-rich food containing most of the wheat's vitamins and minerals (vitamins B and E, and iron) and natural oils. The oils, however, cause the germ to become rancid quickly, so always refrigerate an open jar of wheat germ. Also, if you see it, buy untoasted wheat germ as opposed to the toasted kind. While the toasting may help preserve the germ, it also destroys many of its nutrients, making it a less healthy choice than the raw kind.

Wheat Berries, Cracked Wheat, and Bulgur
All three of these are different forms of the whole-wheat grain, and are all extremely nutritious because they contain the germ and the bran. Added to bread, they all produce an excellent mealy texture and earthy flavor. The difference between these

grains is the way they have been processed, which changes the way you must handle each one prior to adding to your dough.

Wheat berries are the unadulterated whole grain, and must be thoroughly cooked (or soaked in warm water overnight) to soften them before use, otherwise they will pack your dough with gravel-like pellets that are impossible to chew.

Next in size is cracked wheat, which is just as it sounds: the whole-wheat grain, cracked and toasted. Soak cracked wheat in hot water for about an hour before making your bread, or boil briefly until softened. The toasting makes cracked wheat a bit nuttier than regular wheat berries.

Lastly, and probably most commonly found, is bulgur, which is cracked wheat that has also been parboiled, so you do not need to soak it before use. I find this the most convenient of the three, and frequently throw a handful into my whole-grain breads for extra verve.

Rye Flour

Aside from wheat, rye has the next-highest gluten percentage of any flour, although that's not saying much. It is an extremely nutritious grain with a dark, musty flavor. It is also a reliable crop because it can survive even the most adverse growing conditions. Once wheat was discovered to make a better-risen loaf, rye was mostly supplanted around the globe. But in times of famine and climatic change, rye could always be counted upon to yield a bountiful crop.

Bread made with rye is dense, compact, and has a tight-packed crumb. Although it is possible to make a loaf using solely rye flour, the results are much improved with half wheaten-bread flour, or a tablespoon or two of straight gluten. Rye is the flour of choice for dark, Slavic-style pumpernickel bread, not to mention the chewy Jewish seeded rye so necessary for good deli sandwiches.

Cornmeal

Corn is a native American crop that has been prized in this country (especially the south) since the earliest settlers depended upon it for sustenance. Until very recently, however, it was all but ignored in other parts of the world. Cornmeal is available in a rainbow of colors, the most common being yellow, white, and blue. All are pretty much interchangeable, but bread made with blue cornmeal turns a funny gray color that

I don't usually associate with edibles. Yellow and white are much more common, and less expensive, too.

Although corn contains fewer nutrients than many other grains, it has a subtly sweet flavor and a marvelously sandy texture that is a pleasure to consume. Always buy stone-ground cornmeal for the maximum flavor.

Oatmeal

Throughout history, oatmeal has primarily been known as a grain to feed to livestock, or made into gruel in Scotland to fortify Highlanders against the morning chill. Because it contains no gluten, it was never made into bread, although sometimes it was made into flat griddle cakes that need no rising.

Today we favor oatmeal as an addition to wheat breads for its flavor and texture. Oatmeal can be added either cooked or uncooked, but is generally uncooked for the purposes of this book. Buy "old-fashioned" oatmeal, or "rolled oats," but never use "instant" oatmeal, or you will completely lose any speck of texture.

Oat Bran

Like wheat bran, oat bran is the outer covering of the oat groat, and is a gold mine of fiber. Recently, much has been written about oat bran's ability to lower cholesterol and possibly prevent heart attacks. While all this may or may not be true, adding oat bran to bread is a wonderful way to increase fiber in our diets. It also adds extra texture into our breads.

Buckwheat

Buckwheat flourishes in the cooler climates of northern China and Russia. Its protein content is similar to wheat; however, it does not have the necessary gluten to make raised loaves of bread. Buckwheat is used as flour to make pancakes, and is added to wheat bread in small quantities for an unusual depth of flavor. Beware, though, because buckwheat is a strongly flavored grain, and can easily overpower your bread if not added judiciously. Buckwheat groats, otherwise known as kasha, are the whole grain, toasted, and generally cooked in broth or water like rice for a delicious side dish. When onions, mushrooms, and egg noodles are added, the result is the delectable kasha varnischka of Eastern Europe that I absolutely adore as a comforting entrée in the winter. Cooked buckwheat groats can be added to bread for moistness and a woody flavor, and I highly recommend experimenting with this.

Barley
Cultivated since the Stone Age, barley was also thought to have medicinal qualities by the ancient Greeks. A hearty grain, it has been a staple in the diet of most of the world, and was reportedly a fixture for Roman soldiers who carried unleavened cakes of it in sacks while patrolling the empire.

Barley flour has a mild flavor and, when added to wheat breads, makes for a sweet, delicate, cakelike loaf. Toasting the barley flour first in a dry skillet brings out the earthiness of the grain.

Rice
Although rice is the main food source for most of Asia, it is not widely made into bread or even flat cakes. Rice flour has a very high percentage of starch, and is best used in pastry. Brown rice flour makes a nice, light bread with an airy, open crumb and a sweet nutty flavor. Cooked rice is sometimes added to bread for a moist and chewy texture.

Amaranth
Recently discovered in Aztec ruins, amaranth is an ancient grain that is having a modern-day renaissance due to its fruity flavor and terrifically high protein content. You may use either the flour or the cooked grains for an extremely nutritious bread with great flavor and texture.

Millet
Millet is a most digestible, healthy grain that is still a staple in Africa and parts of India, where it is made into delicious flat bread. The flour has no gluten, but combines nicely with wheat for a handsome, yellow loaf. Millet seeds can be added, uncooked, to bread for a crunchy, crumbly texture and pleasant flavor.

Storing Flours and Grains
Flours should be stored airtight in a cool, dark place. The refrigerator or freezer is an ideal place to store flour, if you can afford the space. I store my flour in the cabinet farthest from the stove in large metal cookie tins. In the summertime,

when kitchen insects reproduce prolifically, I sometimes place the tins in resealable plastic bags.

Since whole-grain flours contain the oil-rich germ of the grain, they can become rancid very rapidly. This is especially true if you have bought them from a supermarket, where they may have been sitting on the shelves for weeks, or even months. Make sure the flour you buy is fresh; it should smell clean and perhaps nutty, and look smooth without any distinct lumps. Rancid flour will give an awful mouth-puckering taste to your beautiful bread, so beware.

LEAVENING

Without the aid of some kind of leavening agent, bread dough would be better used for brick laying than for baking. Leavening is what makes the dough rise and lighten, and without it, baked bread would crack teeth. There are different types of leavening that will swell a loaf: yeast, sour starters, and chemical agents such as baking soda and baking powder. Each will create a very different loaf.

Yeast
Yeast is the most typical type of leavening agent for the bread baked in a bread machine. Each teaspoon of yeast is composed of billions of living fungi cells that react with water and carbohydrates to produce carbon dioxide gas. The gas is then trapped by the gluten network and the once solid mass of dough grows porous and fat. Sugar of any kind will nourish the yeast and will increase its carbon dioxide yield, allowing the loaf to rise higher and faster. That is why most recipes call for a tablespoon or so of sugar even if the recipe is not meant to be sweet. Salt will slow down the yeast cells, and acts as a check for overproductive yeast—which can give off so much carbon dioxide that the pressure ruptures the gluten fibers, and all the gas escapes.

Yeast is available in two forms: compressed fresh yeast and dry active yeast. Compressed fresh yeast is sold in cakes and is sometimes known as "cake yeast." It becomes active when mixed with sugar and water, and is a bit faster than dry yeast. It is difficult to find and is not recommended for bread machines.

Dry active yeast, most commonly marketed by Red Star and Fleishmann's, is dehydrated yeast granules that become reactivated when mixed with *warm* water (between 105 and 110 degrees). Hot water will kill the finicky cells, and cold water will leave them dormant. With a bread machine, there is no real worry about mixing the yeast with water of a proper temperature because the machine does this automatically. Proofing the yeast—that is, mixing it with warm water and sugar and letting it sit for several minutes until the mixture begins to ferment and bubble—is not necessary if you use your yeast before it expires (expiration dates are clearly marked on the foil packages). If your dry active yeast turns out to be dry *inactive* yeast, and your dough remains a leaden lump, just set the machine to start and add more yeast (from a different package!). The machine will then knead the new yeast into your bread, and it should rise without a problem.

Yeast can be stored in the refrigerator or freezer, and will keep until it expires.

Sourdough Starters

In ancient times, all bread was made with what we today would call sour starters, for lack of any alternative. Sour starters occur naturally when flour and water are mixed and allowed to ferment. Wild yeasts floating through the air infiltrate the mixture and cause it to seethe and froth. When this is mixed with more flour and baked, raised bread results.

The first risen loaves were thought to be baked by the Egyptians, who saved a piece of old yeast-infested dough to be mixed with new grain for future loaves. Centuries later, when the Romans turned bread baking into an art, they mixed wine with barley grains and left them to ferment. They were then dried out, pulverized, and stored. When it was time to bake bread, this powder was reactivated with water, much like our modern dry active yeast—only much less predictable. The early English achieved the same results using the bubbly foam from fermenting beer, and reportedly their bread was all the lighter for it. However, the characteristic sour flour, which we prize today, was neutralized by the addition of potash.

Sour-tasting dough did not come back into fashion until the pioneers of the Wild West were forced by necessity to revert to ancient practices: saving old dough. Gold miners near San Francisco made sourdough bread famous, and its continued popularity today attests to its addictive flavor.

Today, we are not dependent on the yeasts in sour starters to raise our loaves; packaged yeast ensures this for us. Instead it is the flavor we crave. It is just as easy to make a sour starter as it is to bake bread in a bread machine, so there are no excuses for not trying it. The same starter can be used over and over by simply adding flour and water to the mixture as you remove the amount necessary for your recipe. Tales have it that one family passed a sourdough starter down through generations.

Recipe for Sour Starter:
2 **cups bread flour**
1 **cup warm milk (105–115 degrees)**
1 **cup warm water (105–115 degrees)**
2 **tsp. yeast**
1 **tsp. sugar**

Mix all the ingredients together with an electric mixer until smooth. Place mixture in a bowl and lightly cover with a dish towel or foil. Leave in a warm place for five days to one week, stirring lightly once a day, until the starter is frothy and has a slightly sour smell. If the mixture looks at all pinkish, or if the smell is foul, discard and begin again. Leftover starter should be stored in a jar or container with a tight lid in the refrigerator, and stirred occasionally if you happen to think of it.

Each time you use this starter, you may keep it going by adding a half cup of water, a half cup of milk, and one cup of bread flour to the container and mixing well. Leave the starter out overnight, and then return to the refrigerator for storage. If you do not use the starter very often, after a week or two it will become too sour to use. To maintain the proper balance, every week to ten days take a cup full of starter out and replenish the mixture as described. A properly cared for starter will last for decades, if not longer.

Chemical Agents
Baking powder and baking soda are used in "quick" bread, and do not need kneading or a rising time. Instead they react chemically with the liquid in batters, and carbon dioxide is released, allowing the bread to rise. Sometimes either baking soda or baking powder is added to bread in addition to yeast, as a way of neutralizing acid. In general, however, they are not widely used in the recipes in this book.

LIQUIDS

Liquid is necessary to activate the yeast and bind the loaf. Water, the most basic liquid, will produce a crusty loaf and is used alone for French bread to achieve its characteristic crunchiness. However, bread made with only water will dry out faster than bread made with other liquids, so it is best to plan on making French bread the same day you want to eat it.

Milk, either skimmed, low-fat, or regular, will yield a smoother, more tender interior and a darker crust than plain water. It also lengthens the keeping time of the bread, and adds flavor and aroma. Yeast can feed off of the sugars in milk, and so less added sugar may be called for in a recipe containing milk. In this book, I have used low-fat milk as a standard, but it is perfectly okay to use skimmed or whole milk.

Nonfat dry milk powder mixed with water is another option. It is good to use with the timer because it won't turn when left out overnight in a warm kitchen. Nonfat dry milk improves the structure of the bread by strengthening the gluten in a way that regular milk does not, and so it is sometimes specifically called for in heavier breads that need a stronger gluten network. However, all types of milk add proteins that coagulate under heat and help strengthen the crumb.

Buttermilk is frequently used in bread for its tangy flavor. Like regular milk, it will produce a plush texture and deep color. If you do not have buttermilk, you can substitute regular milk plus one teaspoon vinegar or lemon juice for every cup, but your loaf will not have the same depth of flavor. A better substitute is yogurt stirred with a little milk or water, and used in the same proportions as the buttermilk. Dry buttermilk powder, available in supermarkets and health-food stores, is also fine when mixed with water.

In the days BBM (before bread machines), it was necessary to heat the water to exactly 105 to 115 degrees in order to activate the yeast. If the water was too cold, the yeast wouldn't awaken, or if it was too hot, the yeast would die. Luckily, your bread machine controls the temperature of the dough, and so you needn't bother with all of this. In these recipes I have used plain room-temperature water straight out of the tap and milk directly out of the refrigerator without any problem.

SWEETENERS

Although sugar is not necessary for a loaf of bread, a small amount will increase the yeast's activity and therefore will help raise the dough. If you are on a diet that prohibits sugar, simply leave it out or add just half a teaspoon.

Sweeteners add flavor and color to bread. Brown sugar, molasses, honey, and maple syrup can all be substituted for white sugar. If molasses, honey, or syrup is used, decrease the liquid content of the bread accordingly.

SHORTENING

Some kind of shortening is usually added to breads in small amounts. It contributes flavor and makes the texture tender and flaky. Shortening will also improve the keeping qualities of bread by coating the flour particles, so moisture will not evaporate as quickly. Crispy French breads are made without shortening, but they harden within several hours on account of it.

Butter is the shortening of choice for most bread recipes. Its flavor is wonderful and it is easy to work with. Always buy sweet, unsalted butter as it is made with better quality cream than the salted kind and is apt to be fresher. If you are using a recipe that calls for more than two tablespoons of butter, cut it into small pieces before adding to the bread pan.

Margarine may be substituted for butter, but the flavor will not be as rich. Solid vegetable shortening may also be used.

Oils are frequently called for and may also be substituted for butter if they are the flavorless kind like vegetable. Olive oil should only be used when listed specifically because of its strong, distinct flavor. Choose extra virgin olive oil for the fruitiest taste. Nut oils are very nice when used with the corresponding nut, as in the hazelnut bread on page 71. There, the hazelnut oil adds a mellow undertone and gently reinforces the nut. Nut oils are very perishable, so buy them in small quantities and taste them before baking. Rancid nut oil is a horrible way to ruin a loaf.

All oils should be stored in a cool dark cabinet away from the stove. Oil stored in the refrigerator might congeal, but that will not negatively affect it when brought back to room temperature.

EGGS

Eggs, like milk, add proteins to bread and help build up the structure. The yolk imparts a wonderful richness and a deep yellow hue to the crumb; however, it also contains all the cholesterol and fat. The fat in the yolk will act like any other shortening and help tenderize the loaf. If you wish to limit your cholesterol intake, use egg substitute, or for every egg called for, discard the yolk and use two egg whites instead. The loaf will not have the color and flavor of real eggs, but for most breads in this book it will not matter much. Do not bother using just egg white for the challah recipes—make something else instead or use egg substitute.

Some recipes call for half an egg. If you are watching your cholesterol, this is easy, simply use the egg white. If you would like to use the whole egg, beat it in a bowl first, then measure off two tablespoons (a large egg measures about one quarter cup). Or use two tablespoons of egg substitute.

Use only fresh, grade-A large eggs for the recipes in this book, and make sure to store them in the refrigerator. To see if an egg is fresh, drop it carefully into a pan full of water. If the egg sinks to the bottom, it is fresh. If it bobs on top, throw it out. This is because the longer an egg is exposed to air, the more of it seeps inside the porous shell, which will cause the contents to deteriorate while providing buoyancy.

SALT

Salt is added to bread to bring out the flavor of the grain and to inhibit the yeast. This results in what's called a "well developed" flavor. Use sea salt whenever possible. Bread made without salt tastes flat, so if you are on a low-sodium diet, it is better to reduce the salt in given recipes than to eliminate it.

OTHER ADDITIONS

Fruit, fresh and dried, and nuts are very often added to bread. These should be added during the raisin-bread cycle, if your machine has one, or drop them in the pan five minutes before the end of the kneading cycle. If they are added from the beginning, they will be kneaded into oblivion and become un-detectable to the eye. The flavor will be there, but without any texture.

Aside from the more pedestrian raisins, dates, prunes, and apricots, companies have been experimenting with drying other types of fruit such as blueberries, cherries, and cranberries. These fruits are quickly becoming available in specialty stores and larger supermarkets or they can be ordered by mail from American Spoon Foods (see the Sources List for address and phone number). Use them freely and you will successfully seduce the raisin-bread crowd. A handful of sun-dried tomatoes is another savory idea.

Dried fruits and nuts should be stored airtight in a cool cabinet or in the freezer for longer storage.

Herbs, both fresh and dried, are another common enhancement. Stand fresh herbs in a glass of water as if they were a bouquet of flowers, and they will keep well in the refrigerator for several days (depending on how fresh they were when you bought them). Fresh herbs are the ones I prefer to use because I find the flavor more intense and somewhat sweeter. If you need to substitute dried herbs for fresh, use one third the quantity, as dried are three times more potent. However, dried herbs do lose their flavor over time and should be replaced every two years if you don't use them up before then.

When grated citrus rinds are called for, it is best to mix them with the liquids before adding to the pan, especially if you are using the timer. If the rinds are allowed to dry out, they lose a significant amount of flavor. Use a vegetable peeler to remove only the colored part of the rind (the zest), and avoid the bitter white part underneath (the pith). Then chop the zest finely before adding.

There are a myriad of other ingredients that can be added to bread. Just because you haven't seen a recipe for kiwi-nut bread doesn't mean it's not a good idea. Be creative and you may come up with something not only original, but terrific tasting as well.

UTENSILS

Baking bread, even in the old-fashioned way, does not require many utensils; two strong hands for kneading, counter space, bread pans, measuring cups and spoons, and a nice big bowl in which to rise the dough. With your bread machine, the requirements are tapered down to the barest minimum, but the utensils you do need are important. So, as in the case of ingredients, buy the best you can.

Measuring Cups: Glass measuring cups with a pouring spout are best for measuring liquids; metal cups with handles are convenient for flour because it easy to dip the cup right into the flour bag and sweep off the extra mound on top with a knife. This method is, obviously enough, known as the "dip and sweep" method of measuring. The same term applies with measuring spoons.

Measuring Spoons: It is easiest, when using metal measuring spoons on a ring, to take them off and use them separately; that way you don't have to clean the whole set every time you just need to use the teaspoon. Use the above-described dip-and-sweep method for measuring dry things. When measuring sticky syrups like honey or molasses, and vegetable oil in the same recipe, always measure the vegetable oil first. That way, the syrup will not stick to the spoon.

When a recipe calls for odd-seeming measurements (like one third teaspoon) that do not come with your measuring spoons, an easy way to get the correct amount is to fill the next largest measuring spoon and scoop some of your ingredient out with the point of a butter knife. For example, for one third teaspoon, measure out one half teaspoon and shave a bit off from the top. For one half tablespoon (which can also be measured as one and one half teaspoons) fill the one-tablespoon measure only halfway full. It is perfectly fine to approximate with your eye for these small amounts—a grain or two more or less of wheat germ or salt will not drastically affect your recipe.

Pot Holders: These are essential to use with a bread machine to remove the pan from the machine's belly. The wire handle attached to the pans is deceptively hot, and more than once I have grabbed it firmly, singeing the skin of even *my* "asbestos fingers" (after years of working in the kitchen). Furthermore, when you are shaking the loaf out of the pan, pot holders are essential for removing the kneading pin and firmly holding the sides of the pan while rapping it against the counter, as I usually do to remove stubborn loaves. Finally I trained myself, and now automatically reach for, my trusty pot holder before even opening the hatch.

Cooling Rack: A metal cooling rack is the best way to finish cooling a loaf after it comes out of the bread machine. Get a large size if you don't already own one because you will find yourself using it for all kinds of baking in addition to bread.

Cutting Board: To slice your beautiful loaf in the manner safest to your countertops and knife blades, always cut it on a cutting board, either wooden or plastic.

Serrated Bread Knife: A good-quality serrated knife produces the most even, finest slices, which are ideal for toasting as well as for sandwiches. Cut the loaf with a sawing, back-and-forth motion to avoid squashing the crumb, especially if you are like me and cannot wait for the bread to cool. Of course, you can always tear off large chunks with your hands and munch them quickly, before anyone else wakes up.

Q-Tips: I have had a terrible problem with the kneading paddle getting stuck in the bread pan after I bake a loaf, and sometimes have spent hours trying to remove that tenacious little baton. The best solution I've come up with is using Q-Tips, which are invaluable for greasing the steel rod on which you attach the kneading paddle. Simply moisten the swab with oil and grease both the rod and inside the hole of the kneading paddle. It should stick much less next time. I do this prior to every loaf.

Toothpicks: Sometimes, especially after using the dough cycle, the kneading paddle really holds its ground, assisted by the clumps of pastelike dough clinging in the space where the kneading paddle fits over the steel rod. Inserting wooden toothpicks in this space releases the gook, which you can then scrape out. It is best to do this after you have soaked the pan in warm, soapy water so the offensive dough has the consistency of mere glue rather than cement.

WD-40: Okay, so you've soaked that kneading paddle in several changes of hot water, scraped out the dough schmutz with a toothpick, but the thing refuses to budge. Now it's time for serious measures, and this is when to break out the WD-40, which is an industrial lubricant. Dry the paddle well, and saturate it with WD-40. Allow to sit for a couple of hours, and try to loosen it. This should work—just make sure to wash the paddle very well with soapy water before using it again.

Thick Cotton Kitchen String: Kneading paddles are venomous creatures, and hold a grudge for certain abuses. If yours is seeking revenge for the time you forgot to put the yeast in, you may need some leverage to lift it out. For this I suggest thick, cotton string. Slip it under the paddle, bring it around several times for a strong hold, and use it to help you pull the nasty thing out. This has worked for me very well, and saved my fingertips from the painful twisting necessary to dislodge the mulelike prong.

SOME TIPS FOR USING THE BREAD MACHINE

Here are some things I learned along the way that have since made my bread days even more golden. For tips about how to detach the kneading paddle from the pan, see the above section on utensils.

It is utterly important to get to know the bread-making process occurring in the depths of your machine. Although the instruction manual will probably warn your against peeking inside the hatch, I say that peeking, especially during the kneading period, is necessary for achieving consistently good loaves. Once you know what the dough to a perfect loaf looks like, it is easy to avoid disastrous results. You also will be able to create your own loaf from whatever you have around the house. My standard, everyday bread is nicknamed "mystery loaf" because I can never quite remember what went into it. I just add different grains and liquids until it looks right. Knowing what looks right is the key to bread-machine freedom.

So peek away. Do the ingredients neatly mix up into a smooth, satiny ball that bounces around the machine during the kneading? This is what should happen. Or does the ball stick to the sides of the machine, feel wet and tacky, and relax into the pan's corners when the kneading is finished? This indicates that the dough has too much liquid, and is easily fixed by adding a few tablespoons of flour until it balls up and stops sticking.

Don't overdo the flour or you will get tough clumps of dough that don't come together in a ball, but rather stay somewhat separate as they twist around the machine. During rising, they will look rough, uneven, and floury. To reverse this dryness, just add a bit of water until the dough smoothes out and becomes pliable.

Always make these additions while the machine is kneading so they work themselves right in. Otherwise you will have to remove the dough from the pan, knead them in by hand, and return the corrected lump to rise. But I do not recommend this method except as a last resort, because overkneading the bread will rupture the gluten and the dough won't rise. Also, once the dough is risen, don't peek during the baking or too much heat may escape and alter your loaf.

Sometimes you will notice that the crumb of your bread is soggy and damp. The most common cause of this is leaving the bread in the bread pan too long. After the machine beeps, I usually take the bread out right away and finish cooling it on a rack.

Another cause of this underbaked appearance could be too much sugar in your recipe. Cut down on the sweetener and see if the problem straightens out.

Human error is not necessarily the only reason why your dough may not act perfectly every time and need adjustment. Of course there are times when you will forget to put the yeast in, or add all the ingredients before remembering to put the kneading paddle back in place. But even when you follow through on your part, mishaps can occur, and these flops can be blamed on inconsistencies in the ingredients themselves. Flour is especially wily, and will sometimes not absorb enough liquid to make a smooth dough. This can happen when your kitchen is humid and the flour absorbs the moisture in the air, then having less room for your liquids. Sometimes flour may absorb all the liquid but still need extra to ball up nicely. This occurs mostly in older flour, which has been allowed to sit out and lose its moisture content. Storing flour airtight will help avoid these inconsistencies, but you never know what to expect from the flour you buy. For example, for how long and under what conditions it sat in the grocer's. Get to know your dough, learn how to adjust for the unexpected, and you will have perfect bread (or at least very good bread), almost every time.

Don't be too discouraged if on some days no matter all your effort, your most dependable loaf ends up a doorstop or paperweight. This is the will of the kitchen spirit, or whatever unknown force, and just has to be accepted. Try again later and it will probably turn out fine.

The last tip I would like to offer is what to do with all that leftover bread. Chances are, if you are at all like me, you will want to make fresh bread every few days, even before the last few slices are finished from the old loaf. There are many ways to dispose of these slices: freezing them; making bread crumbs, melba toast, bread pudding, and French toast; feeding the ducks and birds in your neighborhood.

Or what about feeding the hungry people in your neighborhood? Unfortunately, unless you live in a completely rural part of the country, you must know of people who cannot feed themselves. In New York City, where I live, I cannot walk one block without seeing homeless people desperate for food. While testing recipes for this book, I made it a practice to make peanut-butter-and-jelly or cream-cheese sandwiches with the leftover bread and distribute them to the homeless in my neighborhood. If you do not see hungry people on a regular basis, you can get in touch with them through various humanitarian organizations, or your local house of worship.

After all, how much freezer space do you really have?

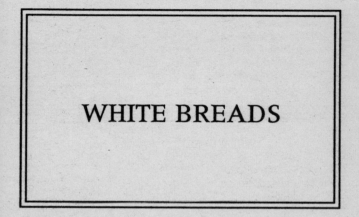

WHITE BREADS

WHITE BREAD

Your basic loaf, good for anything you can think to do with a slice of white bread.

1 lb. Loaf
- ¾ cup milk
- 2 Tbs. butter
- 2 Tbs. sugar
- 1 tsp. salt
- 2½ cups bread flour
- 1½ tsp. yeast

1½ lb. Loaf
- 1 cup milk
- 2½ Tbs. butter
- 3 Tbs. sugar
- 1⅓ tsp. salt
- 3⅓ cups bread flour
- 2½ tsp. yeast

Bake according to manufacturer's instructions.

LUSCIOUS WHITE BREAD

Richer, moister, and more velvety than the basic white bread. This bread is very nice toasted with butter and honey.

1 lb. Loaf
 ¾ cup milk
 1 egg
 2 Tbs. butter
 3 Tbs. sugar
 ½ tsp. salt
 2 cups bread flour
1½ tsp. yeast

1½ lb. Loaf
 1 cup milk
1½ eggs
2½ Tbs. butter
 ¼ cup sugar
 ¾ tsp. salt
 3 cups bread flour
2½ tsp. yeast

Bake according to manufacturer's instructions.

COUNTRY WHITE BREAD

This is a moist, chewy loaf with a slightly crispy crust. Very good with cheese.

1 lb. Loaf
   1 cup water
   1 Tbs. sugar
1½ tsp. salt
   2 cups bread flour
1½ tsp. yeast

1½ lb. Loaf
1½ cups water
1½ Tbs. sugar
   2 tsp. salt
   3 cups bread flour
2½ tsp. yeast

Bake according to manufacturer's instructions.

POTATO BREAD

You can make this light, moist bread with either real, or instant mashed potatoes. It is great for sandwiches.

1 lb. Loaf
- ½ cup milk
- 3 Tbs. butter
- 1 egg
- ⅓ cup mashed potatoes
- 1 Tbs. sugar
- ⅔ tsp. salt
- 2 cups bread flour
- 1½ tsp. yeast

1½ lb. Loaf
- ¾ cup milk
- 4 Tbs. butter
- 1½ eggs
- ½ cup mashed potatoes
- 2 Tbs. sugar
- 1 tsp. salt
- 3 cups bread flour
- 2½ tsp. yeast

Bake according to manufacturer's instructions.

SOUR CREAM BREAD

A delightfully moist bread with an airy texture and impressively tall stature. You may notice that there is no butter or oil in this bread; the sour cream and egg yolk contribute enough fat by themselves.

1 lb. Loaf
   1 cup sour cream
   1 egg
   2 Tbs. sugar
   1 tsp. salt
2½ cups bread flour
1½ tsp. yeast

1½ lb. Loaf
1⅓ cups sour cream
1½ eggs
   3 Tbs. sugar
1⅓ tsp. salt
3½ cups bread flour
2½ tsp. yeast

Bake according to manufacturer's instructions.

BUTTERMILK OAT BREAD

Tangy and moist, try it with a big bowl of soup.

1 lb. Loaf
  1 cup buttermilk
  4 Tbs. butter
  3 Tbs. molasses
  1½ tsp. salt
  1 cup oatmeal
  2 cups bread flour
  1½ tsp. yeast

1½ lb. Loaf
  1⅓ cups buttermilk
  5 Tbs. butter
  4 Tbs. molasses
  2 tsp. salt
  1⅓ cups oatmeal
  2⅔ cups bread flour
  2½ tsp. yeast

Bake according to manufacturer's instructions.

FARMER CHEESE–CINNAMON BREAD

While I was growing up, whenever we had leftover egg noodles in the house my mother would mix them with farmer cheese, cinnamon, and nutmeg for supper the next day. I made up this bread to approximate the flavor of those creamy noodles, which I often crave on rainy days.

1 lb. Loaf
- 1 cup farmer cheese
- ⅓ cup sour cream
- 2 Tbs. butter
- 1 egg
- 3 Tbs. sugar
- ½ tsp. cinnamon
- ½ tsp. freshly grated nutmeg
- ⅔ tsp. salt
- 2½ cups bread flour
- 1½ tsp. yeast

1½ lb. Loaf
- 1¼ cups farmer cheese
- ½ cup sour cream
- 2½ Tbs. butter
- 1½ eggs
- ¼ cup sugar
- ⅔ tsp. cinnamon
- ⅔ tsp. freshly grated nutmeg
- 1 tsp. salt
- 3 cups bread flour
- 2½ tsp. yeast

Bake according to manufacturer's instructions.

SPICED HONEY BREAD

Fragrant with spices, this bread perfumes the whole house. Not too sweet, it makes the most wonderful peanut-butter-and-jelly sandwiches ever!

1 lb. Loaf
⅔ cup water
2 Tbs. milk
3 Tbs. butter
3 Tbs. honey
½ tsp. salt
1 tsp. coriander
½ tsp. cinnamon
½ tsp. anise seeds, crushed
½ tsp. ginger
2⅓ cups bread flour
1½ tsp. yeast

1½ lb. Loaf
¾ cup water
3 Tbs. milk
4 Tbs. butter
¼ cup honey
¾ tsp. salt
1⅓ tsp. coriander
¾ tsp. cinnamon
¾ tsp. anise seeds, crushed
¾ tsp. ginger
3⅛ cups bread flour
2½ tsp. yeast

Bake according to manufacturer's instructions.

IRISH SODA BREAD

Although this bread is not usually made with yeast, this version, adapted for the bread machine, is scrumptious.

1 lb. Loaf
   1 cup buttermilk
   1 Tbs. butter
   2 Tbs. sugar
   1 tsp. salt
   1 tsp. caraway seeds
   ⅓ tsp. baking soda
   2⅓ cups bread flour
   1½ tsp. yeast
   ½ cup currants

1½ lb. Loaf
   1⅓ cups buttermilk
   1½ Tbs. butter
   3 Tbs. sugar
   1½ tsp. salt
   1½ tsp. caraway seeds
   ½ tsp. baking soda
   3 cups bread flour
   2½ tsp. yeast
   ⅔ cup currants

Bake according to manufacturer's instructions, adding the currants during the raisin-bread cycle, or five minutes before the final kneading is finished.

CHALLAH

Although traditionally challah bread is braided, the eggy, rich flavor is the same in any shape. If you have any leftovers (which I rarely seem to), save it for excellent French toast in the morning.

1 lb. Loaf
1 cup water
2½ Tbs. vegetable oil
2 eggs
2 Tbs. sugar
1½ tsp. salt
3 cups bread flour
1½ tsp. yeast

1½ lb. Loaf
1⅓ cups water
3 Tbs. vegetable oil
2½ eggs
3 Tbs. sugar
2 tsp. salt
4 cups bread flour
2½ tsp. yeast

Bake according to manufacturer's instructions.

SEMOLINA BREAD

Semolina flour has a very high gluten content, and therefore makes for an exceptional loaf. Expect a yellow-tinted interior and a well-developed wheat flavor.

1 lb. Loaf
   1 cup water
   1 Tbs. olive oil
   1 tsp. sugar
   1 tsp. salt
1½ cups semolina flour
1½ cups bread flour
1½ tsp. yeast

1½ lb. Loaf
1⅓ cup water
1½ Tbs. olive oil
1½ tsp. sugar
1⅓ tsp. salt
   2 cups semolina flour
   2 cups bread flour
2½ tsp. yeast

Bake according to manufacturer's instructions.

MIXED-GRAIN BREADS

EVERYBODY'S FAVORITE WHOLE WHEAT

This dense, soft bread is really one of the best of its kind.

1 lb. Loaf
- 1 cup water
- 3 Tbs. vegetable oil
- 2 Tbs. molasses
- 1 tsp. salt
- ¼ cup wheat germ
- 1 cup whole-wheat flour
- 1½ cups bread flour
- ¼ cup nonfat dry milk powder
- 1 tsp. gluten
- 1½ tsp. yeast

1½ lb. Loaf
- 1⅓ cups water
- ¼ cup vegetable oil
- 3 Tbs. molasses
- 1½ tsp. salt
- ⅓ cup wheat germ
- 1½ cups whole-wheat flour
- 1¾ cups bread flour
- ⅓ cup nonfat dry milk powder
- 2 tsp. gluten
- 2½ tsp. yeast

Bake according to manufacturer's instructions.

MEALY WHEAT BREAD

Wheat is found four different ways in this toothsome loaf. I adore it toasted for a reviving midmorning snack.

1 lb. Loaf
  1 cup water
  2 Tbs. vegetable oil
  2 Tbs. honey
  1 tsp. salt
  ¼ cup wheat germ
  ¼ cup wheat flakes
  ½ cup bran
  ¾ cup whole-wheat flour
  1½ cups bread flour
  1½ tsp. yeast

1½ lb. Loaf
  1⅓ cups water
  3 Tbs. vegetable oil
  3 Tbs. honey
  1½ tsp. salt
  ⅓ cup wheat germ
  ⅓ cup wheat flakes
  ⅔ cup bran
  1 cup whole-wheat flour
  1⅔ cups bread flour
  2½ tsp. yeast

Bake according to manufacturer's instructions.

WHOLE-WHEAT IRISH SODA BREAD

A more nutritious, denser soda bread than usual.

1 lb. Loaf
  1 cup buttermilk
  1 Tbs. butter
  2 Tbs. sugar
  1 tsp. salt
  1 tsp. caraway seeds
  ⅓ tsp. baking soda
  1 cup whole-wheat flour
  1⅓ cups bread flour
  1½ tsp. yeast
  ½ cup currants

1½ lb. Loaf
  1⅓ cup buttermilk
  1½ Tbs. butter
  3 Tbs. sugar
  1½ tsp. salt
  1½ tsp. caraway seeds
  ½ tsp. baking soda
  1¼ cups whole-wheat flour
  1¾ cups bread flour
  2½ tsp. yeast
  ⅔ cup currants

Bake according to manufacturer's instructions, adding the currants during the raisin-bread cycle, or five minutes before the final kneading is finished.

FIVE-GRAIN HEALTH BREAD

This flavorful, fibrous bread is my favorite whole grain loaf. It keeps marvelously and travels well, making it an ideal gift.

1 lb. Loaf
1 cup water
3 Tbs. vegetable oil
2 Tbs. honey
1 tsp. salt
2 Tbs. flax seeds
¼ cup wheat germ
¼ cup buckwheat flour
½ cup oatmeal
½ cup whole-wheat flour
1½ cups bread flour
1½ tsp. yeast
¼ cup sunflower seeds

1½ lb. Loaf
1⅓ cups water
¼ cup vegetable oil
3 Tbs. honey
1½ tsp. salt
3 Tbs. flax seeds
⅓ cup wheat germ
⅓ cup buckwheat flour
¾ cup minus 1 Tbs. oatmeal
¾ cup minus 1 Tbs. whole-wheat flour
2 cups bread flour
2½ tsp. yeast
⅓ cup sunflower seeds

Bake according to manufacturer's instructions, adding the sunflower seeds during the raisin-bread cycle, or five minutes before the final kneading is finished.

BOSTON BROWN BREAD

Although this bread is generally steamed for hours, the bread machine produces a very credible rendition.

1 lb. Loaf
  1 cup water
  3 Tbs. vegetable oil
  3 Tbs. molasses
  ¾ tsp. salt
  1 Tbs. unsweetened cocoa
  ½ cup cornmeal
  ½ cup whole-wheat flour
  ½ cup rye flour
  1½ cups bread flour
  2 Tbs. nonfat dry milk powder
  2 tsp. yeast
  ½ cup raisins

1½ lb. Loaf
  1⅓ cups water
  ¼ cup vegetable oil
  ¼ cup molasses
  1 tsp. salt
  1½ Tbs. unsweetened cocoa
  ⅔ cup cornmeal
  ⅔ cup whole-wheat flour
  1⅔ cup rye flour
  2 cups bread flour
  3 Tbs. nonfat dry milk powder
  2½ tsp. yeast
  ¾ cup raisins

Bake according to manufacturer's instructions, adding the raisins during the raisin-bread cycle, or five minutes before the final kneading is finished.

WHOLE-GRAIN NUT BREAD

You may use any combination of nuts for this yeast-scented, dense loaf.

1 lb. Loaf
    1 cup water
    3 Tbs. vegetable oil, or nut oil of your choice
    1 Tbs. sugar
    1 tsp. salt
    ¼ cup wheat germ
    ½ cup rye flour
    ¾ cup whole-wheat flour
    1½ cups bread flour
    1½ tsp. yeast
    ¼ cup walnuts, chopped
    2 Tbs. cashews, chopped
    2 Tbs. Brazil nuts, chopped

1½ lb. Loaf
    1⅓ cups water
    ¼ cup vegetable oil, or nut oil of your choice
    1½ Tbs. sugar
    1½ tsp. salt
    ⅓ cup wheat germ
    ⅔ cup rye flour
    1 cup whole-wheat flour
    2 cups bread flour
    2½ tsp. yeast
    ⅓ cup walnuts, chopped
    3 Tbs. cashews, chopped
    3 Tbs. Brazil nuts, chopped

Bake according to manufacturer's instructions, adding the nuts during the raisin-bread cycle, or five minutes before the final kneading is finished.

WALNUT BEER BREAD

This loaf was favorite before my bread machine, and is now even easier to make. Great with cheese!

1 lb. Loaf
  1 cup beer
  2 Tbs. walnut oil
  1 Tbs. molasses
  1 tsp. salt
  ⅔ tsp. rosemary
  1½ cups whole-wheat flour
  1½ cups bread flour
  1½ tsp. yeast
  ½ cup walnuts, chopped
  ⅓ cup sauteed onions

1½ lb. Loaf
1⅓ cups beer
  3 Tbs. walnut oil
1½ Tbs. molasses
1½ tsp. salt
  ¾ tsp. rosemary
  2 cups whole-wheat flour
  2 cups bread flour
2½ tsp. yeast
  ⅔ cup walnuts, chopped
  ½ cup sauteed onions

Bake according to manufacturer's instructions, adding the walnuts and onions during the raisin-bread cycle, or five minutes before the final kneading is finished.

CURRANT WALNUT WHEAT BREAD

This outstanding bread is not sweet, but moist and flavorful nonetheless. Toasting the walnuts first brings out their flavor and aroma.

1 lb. Loaf
- ⅓ cup walnuts
- 1 cup water
- 2 Tbs. walnut oil
- 1 Tbs. sugar
- 1 tsp. salt
- 1½ cups whole-wheat flour
- 1½ cups bread flour
- 1½ tsp. yeast
- ⅓ cup currants

1½ lb. Loaf
- ½ cup walnuts
- 1¼ cups water
- 3 Tbs. walnut oil
- 1½ Tbs. sugar
- 1½ tsp. salt
- 2 cups whole-wheat flour
- 2 cups bread flour
- 2½ tsp. yeast
- ½ cup currants

Put walnuts in a hot skillet over high heat, and stir constantly until they take on a deep golden color and release their scent. Watch very closely—they can burn easily. When cool, chop coarsely, and set aside with the currants.

Place other ingredients in the bread pan, and bake according to manufacturer's instructions, adding the currants and walnuts during the raisin-bread cycle, or five minutes before the final kneading is finished.

MILLET BREAD

A crunchy, yeasty bread that slices perfectly and is ideal for sandwiches.

1 lb. Loaf
   1 cup water
   2 Tbs. vegetable oil
   1 tsp. sugar
   1 tsp. salt
   ½ cup millet seeds
   1 cup millet flour
   1½ cups bread flour
   1½ tsp. yeast

1½ lb. Loaf
   1⅓ cup water
   3 Tbs. vegetable oil
   1½ tsp. sugar
   1⅓ tsp. salt
   ¾ cup millet seeds
   1¼ cups millet flour
   2 cups bread flour
   2½ tsp. yeast

Bake according to manufacturer's instructions.

BROWN RICE BREAD

A delicate, well-risen loaf with a sandy texture and pale, off-white color. It goes particularly well with peanut butter, making it a most nutritious meal. Brown rice flour is available in health-food stores.

1 lb. Loaf
   1 cup water
   2 Tbs. vegetable oil
   1 tsp. sugar
   1 tsp. salt
   ½ cup brown rice, cooked
   1 cup brown rice flour
   1½ cups bread flour
   1½ tsp. yeast

1½ lb. Loaf
   1⅓ cup water
   3 Tbs. vegetable oil
   1½ tsp. sugar
   1⅓ tsp. salt
   ¾ cup brown rice, cooked
   1¼ cups brown rice flour
   2 cups bread flour
   2½ tsp. yeast

Bake according to manufacturer's instructions.

TRIPLE BARLEY BREAD

Barley is used in three forms for this bread: the flour, syrup form, and cooked grains all combine to form a dense, very moist, muffinlike bread. Golden raisins, added with the cooked barley grains on the raisin-bread cycle, add a tart touch.

1 lb. Loaf
   1 cup water
   2 Tbs. butter
   ¼ cup barley malt syrup
   ⅓ cup sugar
   1½ tsp. salt
   1 tsp. cinnamon
   ½ cup barley flour
   2½ cups bread flour
   1½ Tbs. nonfat dry milk powder
   1½ tsp. yeast
   1 cup cooked barley
   ¾ cup golden raisins (optional)

1½ lb. Loaf
   1⅓ cups water
   2½ Tbs. butter
   ¼ cup barley malt syrup
   ½ cup sugar
   2 tsp. salt
   1½ tsp. cinnamon
   ⅔ cup barley flour
   3⅓ cups bread flour
   2 Tbs. nonfat dry milk powder
   2½ tsp. yeast
   1½ cups cooked barley
   1¼ cups golden raisins (optional)

Bake according to manufacturer's instructions, adding the barley and optional raisins during the raisin-bread cycle, or five minutes before the final kneading is finished.

SPELT BREAD

Spelt is an ancient variant of wheat and was one of the first grains ever made into raised loaves. Although it is difficult to procure, if you do find some (large health-food stores are a good bet), buy as much as you can because it produces a flavorful, fabulously chewy loaf without the heaviness of most whole grains.

1 lb. Loaf
1 cup water
2 Tbs. vegetable oil
3 Tbs. honey
1 tsp. salt
1½ cups spelt flour
1½ cups bread flour
1½ tsp. yeast

1½ lb. Loaf
1⅓ cups water
3 Tbs. vegetable oil
¼ cup honey
1½ tsp. salt
2 cups spelt flour
2 cups bread flour
2½ tsp. yeast

Bake according to manufacturer's instructions.

EXTRA SOY BREAD

Many of my friends were shocked to learn of the healthy ingredients in this delicious bread. Soy nuts are actually dry-roasted soy beans, which taste and look a little like peanuts. Find them in health-food stores, or substitute peanuts for an interesting variation.

1 lb. Loaf
- 1 cup soy milk
- 1½ Tbs. vegetable oil
- 3 Tbs. honey
- ⅔ tsp. salt
- 1 cup soy flour
- 1½ cups bread flour
- 1½ tsp. yeast
- ½ cup soy nuts

1½ lb. Loaf
- 1⅓ cups soy milk
- 2 Tbs. vegetable oil
- ¼ cup honey
- 1 tsp. salt
- 1⅓ cups soy flour
- 2 cups bread flour
- 2½ tsp. yeast
- ⅔ cup soy nuts

Bake according to manufacturer's instructions, adding the soy nuts during the raisin-bread cycle, or five minutes before the final kneading is finished.

CORN BREAD

This moist, nubby bread is super when toasted with cinnamon and honey smeared on. Use frozen corn kernels if you cannot get fresh ears; in which case you will not need to cook them.

1 lb. Loaf
   1 cup milk
   4 Tbs. butter
   1 egg
   3 Tbs. honey
   1 tsp. salt
   1 cup cornmeal
   2 cups bread flour
1½ tsp. yeast
   ½ cup cooked corn kernels

1½ lb. Loaf
1⅓ cups milk
   5 Tbs. butter
1½ eggs
   ¼ cup honey
1½ tsp. salt
1½ cups cornmeal
2½ cups bread flour
2½ tsp. yeast
   ⅔ cup cooked corn kernels

Bake according to manufacturer's instructions, adding the corn during the raisin-bread cycle, or five minutes before the final kneading is finished.

SEEDED RYE BREAD

A perfect deli loaf—break out the pastrami!

1 lb. Loaf
- ⅞ cup water
- 1 Tbs. vegetable oil
- 1½ Tbs. molasses
- 1 tsp. salt
- 1 Tbs. caraway seeds
- 1 cup rye flour
- 1¾ cups bread flour
- 3 Tbs. nonfat dry milk powder
- 1½ tsp. yeast

1½ lb. Loaf
- 1⅛ cups water
- 1½ Tbs. vegetable oil
- 2 Tbs. molasses
- 1½ tsp. salt
- 1½ Tbs. caraway seeds
- 1⅓ cups rye flour
- 2⅓ cups bread flour
- ¼ cup nonfat dry milk powder
- 2½ tsp. yeast

Bake according to manufacturer's instructions.

ORANGE RYE BREAD

Brightly flavored with orange peel, this rye is wonderful with cocktails, or make mustard cheese sandwiches with thin slices of it.

1 lb. Loaf
- ⅞ cup orange juice
- 1 Tbs. vegetable oil
- 3 Tbs. honey
- 1½ tsp. salt
- 1 Tbs. caraway seeds
- 1 tsp. grated orange rind
- 1 cup rye flour
- 1½ cups bread flour
- 1½ tsp. yeast

1½ lb. Loaf
- 1⅛ cups orange juice
- 1½ Tbs. vegetable oil
- ¼ cup honey
- 2 tsp. salt
- 1½ Tbs. caraway seeds
- 1½ tsp. grated orange rind
- 1⅓ cups rye flour
- 2 cups bread flour
- 2½ tsp. yeast

Bake according to manufacturer's instructions.

SWEDISH RYE BREAD

My Swedish friend Max, a self-proclaimed rye-bread fanatic, claims that this bread compares favorably with the ones he enjoyed as a boy in Lund. It is brightly flavored with fennel and orange peel. Serve thin slices with cocktails and good herring.

1 lb. Loaf
   1 cup water
   2 Tbs. vegetable oil
   2 Tbs. honey
   1 tsp. salt
   1 tsp. fennel seeds
   1 tsp. caraway seeds
1½ tsp. grated orange rind
1¼ cups rye flour
1½ cups bread flour
1½ tsp. yeast

1½ lb. Loaf
1⅓ cups water
2½ Tbs. vegetable oil
   3 Tbs. honey
1½ tsp. salt
1½ tsp. fennel seeds
1½ tsp. caraway seeds
   2 tsp. grated orange rind
1¾ cups rye flour
   2 cups bread flour
2½ tsp. yeast

Bake according to manufacturer's instructions.

PEANUT BUTTER–ONION
RYE BREAD

A twist on the classic rye bread to be sure. This bread has a
subtle peanut flavor and an especially nice texture.

1 lb. Loaf
   1 cup water
   2 Tbs. vegetable oil
   ½ cup peanut butter
   2 Tbs. onion, chopped
   1 Tbs. caraway seeds
   1 tsp. salt
   1 cup rye flour
1½ cups bread flour
   2 Tbs. nonfat dry milk powder
1½ tsp. yeast

1½ lb. Loaf
1⅓ cups water
   3 Tbs. vegetable oil
   ⅔ cup peanut butter
   3 Tbs. onion, chopped
1½ Tbs. caraway seeds
1½ tsp. salt
1⅓ cup rye flour
   2 cups bread flour
   3 Tbs. nonfat dry milk powder
2½ tsp. yeast

Bake according to manufacturer's instructions.

SOUR CHERRY RYE BREAD

Dried sour cherries are rapidly becoming available in specialty stores, and their sweet-tart flavor adds zest to this rye bread.

1 lb. Loaf
- 1 cup water
- 2 Tbs. vegetable oil
- 2 Tbs. molasses
- ¾ tsp. salt
- 1½ Tbs. unsweetened cocoa
- 1 Tbs. caraway seeds
- 1½ cups rye flour
- 1½ cups bread flour
- 2 Tbs. nonfat dry milk powder
- 2 tsp. yeast
- ½ cup dried sour cherries

1½ lb. Loaf
- 1⅓ cups water
- 2½ Tbs. vegetable oil
- 3 Tbs. molasses
- 1 tsp. salt
- 2 Tbs. unsweetened cocoa
- 1½ Tbs. caraway seeds
- 2 cups rye flour
- 2 cups bread flour
- 2 Tbs. nonfat dry milk powder
- 2½ tsp. yeast
- ¾ cup dried sour cherries

Bake according to manufacturer's instructions, adding the dried sour cherries during the raisin-bread cycle, or five minutes before the final kneading is finished.

SOUR CREAM–RYE FLAKE BREAD

This chewy bread combines rye flour and rye flakes with sour cream for a tasty, sweet bread that keeps very well. Rye flakes are available in most health-food stores, but if you cannot find them, you may substitute oatmeal.

1 lb. Loaf
- 1 cup sour cream
- 1 Tbs. vegetable oil
- 3 Tbs. honey
- ⅔ tsp. salt
- ½ cup rye flakes
- ½ cup rye flour
- 1½ cups bread flour
- 1½ tsp. yeast

1½ lb. Loaf
- 1⅓ cups sour cream
- 1½ Tbs. vegetable oil
- ¼ cup honey
- 1 tsp. salt
- ⅔ cup rye flakes
- ⅔ cup rye flour
- 2 cups bread flour
- 2½ tsp. yeast

Bake according to manufacturer's instructions.

PUMPERNICKEL BREAD

This version of pumpernickel yields a dark, flavorful loaf.

1 lb. Loaf
- 1 cup water
- 3 Tbs. strong coffee
- 2 Tbs. vegetable oil
- 2 Tbs. molasses
- 2 Tbs. unsweetened cocoa
- ½ tsp. salt
- 1½ Tbs. caraway seeds
- ⅔ cup cornmeal
- 1 cup rye flour
- 1½ cups bread flour
- 2 tsp. yeast

1½ lb. Loaf
- 1¼ cups water
- ¼ cup strong coffee
- 2½ Tbs. vegetable oil
- 3 Tbs. molasses
- 3 Tbs. unsweetened cocoa
- ¾ tsp. salt
- 2 Tbs. caraway seeds
- ¾ cup cornmeal
- 1¼ cups rye flour
- 1¾ cups bread flour
- 2½ tsp. yeast

Bake according to manufacturer's instructions.

RUSSIAN BLACK BREAD

This handsome, stately loaf, with its deep molasses flavor and chewy interior, tastes great in any manner you care to eat it.

1 lb. Loaf

- ¼ cup apple cider
- ¾ cup water
- 2 Tbs. vegetable oil
- 1 Tbs. cider vinegar
- ¼ cup onions, chopped
- 1 Tbs. molasses
- 1 tsp. salt
- 2 Tbs. unsweetened cocoa
- 1 tsp. instant coffee powder
- 1 Tbs. caraway seeds
- 1 tsp. sesame seeds
- ⅛ tsp. fennel seeds
- ¼ cup wheat germ
- ¼ cup whole-wheat flour
- 1 cup rye flour
- 1½ cups bread flour
- 1½ tsp. yeast

1½ lb. Loaf

- ⅓ cup apple cider
- 1 cup water
- 2½ Tbs. vegetable oil
- 1½ Tbs. cider vinegar
- ⅓ cup onions, chopped
- 1½ Tbs. molasses
- 1½ tsp. salt
- 2½ Tbs. unsweetened cocoa
- 1½ tsp. instant coffee powder
- 1½ Tbs. caraway seeds
- 1½ tsp. sesame seeds
- ¼ tsp. fennel seeds
- ⅓ cup wheat germ
- ⅓ cup whole-wheat flour
- 1⅓ cups rye flour
- 2 cups bread flour
- 2½ tsp. yeast

Bake according to manufacturer's instructions.

ANADAMA BREAD

There are as many versions of how this bread got its name as there are versions of the recipe itself. Let's just say that sometime during the early colonial period in America, a woman named Anna was too enthusiastic about cornmeal, and used the indigenous grain without discretion. Her grouchy husband, grown weary of the cornmeal gruel Anna daily dished out, insisted she make a loaf of bread. Not wanting to forgo her new favorite, Anna made the loaf with—guess what. Upon tasting the hated grain in his slice, her husband was so angry that for weeks he walked around the village muttering "Anna, damn her."

1 lb. Loaf
　1 cup milk, scalded
　¾ cup cornmeal
　3 Tbs. vegetable oil
　¼ cup molasses
　1 tsp. salt
　½ cup whole-wheat flour
1½ cups bread flour
1½ tsp. yeast

1½ lb. Loaf
1¼ cup milk, scalded
　1 cup cornmeal
　¼ cup vegetable oil
　⅓ cup molasses
1½ tsp. salt
　⅔ cup whole-wheat flour
　2 cups bread flour
2½ tsp. yeast

Add the cornmeal to the hot milk, and let sit until the mixture reaches room temperature. Add all the ingredients to the bread pan, and bake according to manufacturer's instructions.

MAPLE PECAN BREAD

A superb loaf that harmoniously unites luscious New England maple syrup with America's favorite southern nut.

1 lb. Loaf
- ⅔ cup water
- ¼ cup maple syrup
- 1½ Tbs. butter
- 1 tsp. salt
- ½ cup oatmeal
- ½ cup whole-wheat flour
- 2 cups bread flour
- 2 Tbs. nonfat dry milk powder
- 1½ tsp. yeast
- ½ cup pecan halves

1½ lb. Loaf
- 1 cup water
- ⅓ cup maple syrup
- 2 Tbs. butter
- 1½ tsp. salt
- ¾ cup oatmeal
- ¾ cup whole-wheat flour
- 2½ cups bread flour
- 3 Tbs. nonfat dry milk powder
- 2½ tsp. yeast
- ⅔ cup pecan halves

Bake according to manufacturer's instructions, adding the pecan halves during the raisin-bread cycle, or five minutes before the final kneading is finished.

MOLASSES BREAD

A superb, dark brown loaf with a velvet crumb.

1 lb. Loaf
 ¾ cup milk
 3 Tbs. vegetable oil
 ⅓ cup molasses
 1 Tbs. instant espresso powder
 1 tsp. salt
 ¾ cup oatmeal
 ¾ cup whole-wheat flour
1½ cups bread flour
1½ tsp. yeast

1½ lb. Loaf
 1 cup milk
 ¼ cup vegetable oil
 ½ cup molasses
1½ Tbs. instant espresso powder
1½ tsp. salt
 1 cup oatmeal
 1 cup whole-wheat flour
 2 cups bread flour
2½ tsp. yeast

Bake according to manufacturer's instructions.

AROMATIC SEED BREAD

A fragrant, enticing loaf that keeps very well.

1 lb. Loaf
   1 cup water
   2 Tbs. vegetable oil
   3 Tbs. molasses
   ½ tsp. salt
   ½ tsp. fennel seeds
   ½ tsp. anise seeds
   2 tsp. caraway seeds
   ¼ tsp. celery seeds
   ⅔ cup oatmeal
   1 cup rye flour
1½ cups bread flour
   2 tsp. yeast

1½ lb. Loaf
1¼ cups water
2½ Tbs. vegetable oil
   ¼ cup molasses
   ¾ tsp. salt
   ⅔ tsp. fennel seeds
   ⅔ tsp. anise seeds
   1 Tbs. caraway seeds
   ⅓ tsp. celery seeds
   ¾ cup oatmeal
1¼ cups rye flour
1¾ cups bread flour
2½ tsp. yeast

Bake according to manufacturer's instructions.

SESAME CASHEW BREAD

This crunchy bread can be made with any nut you happen to have on hand. Unblanched almonds are a favorite variant of mine.

1 lb. Loaf
⅓ cup sesame seeds
⅓ cup cashews, finely chopped
1 cup water
1 Tbs. vegetable oil
1 Tbs. sesame oil
2 Tbs. brown sugar
1 tsp. salt
1½ cups whole-wheat flour
1½ cups bread flour
2 Tbs. nonfat dry milk powder
1½ tsp. yeast

1½ lb. Loaf
½ cup sesame seeds
½ cup cashews, finely chopped
1¼ cups water
1½ Tbs. vegetable oil
1½ Tbs. sesame oil
3 Tbs. brown sugar
1½ tsp. salt
2 cups whole-wheat flour
2 cups bread flour
3 Tbs. nonfat dry milk powder
2½ tsp. yeast

Place sesame seeds and cashews in a hot skillet over high heat, and stir constantly until they take on a pale golden color. Watch very closely—these burn easily.

Put other ingredients in the bread pan, and bake according to manufacturer's instructions, adding the cashews and sesame seeds during the raisin-bread cycle, or five minutes before the final kneading is finished.

TOASTED SESAME–BARLEY BREAD

Toasting the sesame seeds and barley grains makes for a surprisingly nutty loaf with a pleasant mealy crumb.

1 lb. Loaf
 ¼ **cup sesame seeds**
 ½ **cup barley grains**
 1 **cup water**
 1 **Tbs. vegetable oil**
 1 **Tbs. sesame oil**
 2 **Tbs. honey**
 1 **tsp. salt**
 ¾ **cup barley flour**
 1½ **cups bread flour**
 2 **Tbs. nonfat dry milk powder**
 1½ **tsp. yeast**

1½ lb. Loaf
 ⅓ **cup sesame seeds**
 ⅔ **cup barley grains**
 1¼ **cups water**
 1½ **Tbs. vegetable oil**
 1½ **Tbs. sesame oil**
 3 **Tbs. honey**
 1½ **tsp. salt**
 1 **cup barley flour**
 3 **cups bread flour**
 3 **Tbs. nonfat dry milk powder**
 2½ **tsp. yeast**

Place sesame seeds and barley in a preheated skillet over high heat, and stir constantly until they take on a pale golden color. Watch closely—these burn very easily. When cool, grind in a food processor or blender until they feel powdery. Add to the bread pan with the flours, and bake according to manufacturer's instructions.

OAT BRAN BREAD

Dense, chewy, yeasty, and healthy. What a combination!

1 lb. Loaf
   1 cup water
   2 Tbs. vegetable oil
   2 Tbs. molasses
   1 tsp. salt
   1 cup oat bran
   ¾ cup whole-wheat flour
1½ cups bread flour
   ¼ cup nonfat dry milk powder
   1 Tbs. gluten
1½ tsp. yeast

1½ lb. Loaf
1⅓ cups water
   3 Tbs. vegetable oil
   3 Tbs. molasses
1½ tsp. salt
1⅓ cups oat bran
   1 cup whole-wheat flour
1⅔ cups bread flour
   ⅓ cup nonfat dry milk powder
1½ Tbs. gluten
2½ tsp. yeast

Bake according to manufacturer's instructions.

OATMEAL HONEY BREAD

A homey, soft, not-too-sweet bread that is just fine served plain, with a nice glass of milk or cup of tea.

1 lb. Loaf
   1 cup milk
   1 egg
   2 Tbs. butter
   2 Tbs. honey
   1 tsp. salt
   1 cup oatmeal
1½ cups bread flour
1½ tsp. yeast

1½ lb. Loaf
1⅓ cups milk
1½ eggs
2½ Tbs. butter
   3 Tbs. honey
1⅓ tsp. salt
1½ cups oatmeal
   2 cups bread flour
2½ tsp. yeast

Bake according to manufacturer's instructions.

HAZELNUT APRICOT OAT BREAD

A sophisticated dried-fruit-and-nut bread that deserves the finest creamery butter as an accompaniment. This dough also makes excellent dinner rolls.

1 lb. Loaf
- 1 cup water
- 2 Tbs. hazelnut or vegetable oil
- 1 Tbs. sugar
- 1 tsp. salt
- ½ cup oatmeal
- 1 cup whole-wheat flour
- 1½ cups bread flour
- 2 Tbs. nonfat dry milk powder
- 1½ tsp. yeast
- ⅓ cup dried apricots, chopped
- ⅓ cup hazelnuts, chopped

1½ lb. Loaf
- 1¼ cups water
- 3 Tbs. hazelnut or vegetable oil
- 1½ Tbs. sugar
- 1½ tsp. salt
- ¾ cup oatmeal
- 1¼ cups whole-wheat flour
- 2 cups bread flour
- 3 Tbs. nonfat dry milk powder
- 2½ tsp. yeast
- ½ cup dried apricots, chopped
- ½ cup hazelnuts, chopped

Bake according to manufacturer's instructions, adding the apricots and hazelnuts during the raisin-bread cycle, or five minutes before the final kneading is finished.

PEANUT BUTTER HONEY OATMEAL BREAD

When I first made this loaf, I put the ingredients into the bread pan, turned the machine on, and left the house for the whole morning. When I returned home, I found a chunk from the top of the loaf missing, and a note stuck inside the bread machine from my neighbor across the hall who keeps a set of my keys: "I could smell this from my apartment, and it smelled so amazing that I had to come over and steal some immediately!! Thanks!" You're welcome, Molly.

1 lb. Loaf
  1 **cup water**
1½ **Tbs. butter**
  ½ **cup peanut butter**
  ½ **cup honey**
  1 **tsp. salt**
  1 **cup oatmeal**
  2 **cups bread flour**
1½ **tsp. yeast**

1½ lb. Loaf
1⅓ **cups water**
  2 **Tbs. butter**
  ⅔ **cup peanut butter**
  ⅔ **cup honey**
1⅓ **tsp. salt**
1⅓ **cups oatmeal**
2⅔ **cups bread flour**
2½ **tsp. yeast**

Bake according to manufacturer's instructions.

BUCKWHEAT BREAD

This moist loaf is best toasted. Buckwheat groats, also known as kasha, impart a marvelous depth of flavor to this earthy bread.

1 lb. Loaf
- ⅞ cup water
- 3 Tbs. vegetable oil
- ¼ cup buckwheat groats, cooked
- 2 Tbs. molasses
- 1 tsp. salt
- ¼ cup wheat germ
- ¼ cup whole-wheat flour
- ½ cup buckwheat flour
- 2 cups bread flour
- 3 Tbs. nonfat dry milk powder
- 1½ tsp. yeast

1½ lb. Loaf
- 1 cup water
- ¼ cup vegetable oil
- ⅓ cup buckwheat groats, cooked
- 3 Tbs. molasses
- 1½ tsp. salt
- ⅓ cup wheat germ
- ⅓ cup whole-wheat flour
- ⅔ cup buckwheat flour
- 2⅔ cups bread flour
- ¼ cup nonfat dry milk powder
- 2½ tsp. yeast

Bake according to manufacturer's instructions.

BRAN CEREAL BREAD

Full of fiber, yet moist and lush. Very good for breakfast.

1 lb. Loaf
  1 cup milk
  3 Tbs. vegetable oil
  2 Tbs. honey
1½ tsp. salt
  ¼ cup wheat germ
  ¾ cup bran cereal
  2 cups bread flour
  1 Tbs. nonfat dry milk powder
1½ tsp. yeast

1½ lb. Loaf
1⅓ cups milk
  ¼ cup vegetable oil
  3 Tbs. honey
  2 tsp. salt
  ⅓ cup wheat germ
  1 cup bran cereal
2⅔ cups bread flour
  2 Tbs. nonfat dry milk powder
2½ tsp. yeast

Bake according to manufacturer's instructions.

DATE-NUT BRAN BREAD

My grandmother used to make date-nut bran muffins for my sister and me, and so inspired this bread. Sandwich cream cheese between the slices for a delicious lunch or snack.

1 lb. Loaf
  1 cup water
  2 Tbs. vegetable oil
  2 Tbs. molasses
  2 tsp. instant coffee powder
  1 Tbs. grated orange rind
  1 tsp. salt
  ½ cup bran
  ½ cup whole-wheat flour
  1½ cups bread flour
  3 Tbs. nonfat dry milk powder
  1½ tsp. yeast
  ⅓ cup dates, chopped
  ⅓ cup walnuts, chopped

1½ lb. Loaf
  1⅓ cups water
  3 Tbs. vegetable oil
  3 Tbs. molasses
  1 Tbs. instant coffee powder
  1½ Tbs. grated orange rind
  1½ tsp. salt
  ⅔ cup bran
  ⅔ cup whole-wheat flour
  2 cups bread flour
  ¼ cup nonfat dry milk powder
  1½ tsp. yeast
  ½ cup dates, chopped
  ½ cup walnuts, chopped

Bake according to manufacturer's instructions, adding the dates and nuts during the raisin-bread cycle, or five minutes before the final kneading is finished.

PRUNE BRAN BREAD

This moist loaf is superior when fresh, but even better toasted the next day.

1 lb. Loaf
  1 cup prune juice
  2 Tbs. vegetable oil
  2 Tbs. molasses
  1 Tbs. grated lemon rind
  1 tsp. salt
  ½ cup bran
  ½ cup whole-wheat flour
  1½ cups bread flour
  ¼ cup nonfat dry milk powder
  1½ tsp. yeast
  ⅔ cup prunes, chopped

1½ lb. Loaf
1⅓ cups prune juice
  3 Tbs. vegetable oil
  3 Tbs. molasses
1½ Tbs. grated lemon rind
1½ tsp. salt
  ⅔ cup bran
  ⅔ cup whole-wheat flour
  2 cups bread flour
  ⅓ cup nonfat dry milk powder
2½ tsp. yeast
  ¾ cup prunes, chopped

Bake according to manufacturer's instructions, adding the prunes during the raisin-bread cycle, or five minutes before the final kneading is finished.

APPLESAUCE BRAN BREAD

A nutritious loaf, moister than most because of the applesauce.

1 lb. Loaf
1¼ cups unsweetened applesauce
2 Tbs. vegetable oil
3 Tbs. molasses
1 tsp. salt
¾ cup bran
¾ cup whole-wheat flour
1½ cups bread flour
1½ tsp. yeast

1½ lb. Loaf
1⅓ cups unsweetened applesauce
3 Tbs. vegetable oil
¼ cup molasses
1½ tsp. salt
1 cup bran
1 cup whole-wheat flour
2 cups bread flour
2½ tsp. yeast

Bake according to manufacturer's instructions.

AMARANTH DATE BREAD

The idea for this protein-packed bread was given to me by my friend Vivian, who bakes a delicious quick bread version. It has a pleasant mealy texture, and keeps very well.

1 lb. Loaf
1 cup water
3 Tbs. vegetable oil
2 Tbs. sugar
1½ tsp. salt
½ cup cooked amaranth grains
¼ cup amaranth flour
2 cups bread flour
1½ tsp. yeast
½ cup dates, chopped

1½ lb. Loaf
1⅓ cups water
¼ cup vegetable oil
3 Tbs. sugar
2 tsp. salt
¾ cup cooked amaranth grains
½ cup amaranth flour
2⅔ cups bread flour
2½ tsp. yeast
¾ cup dates, chopped

Bake according to manufacturer's instructions, adding the dates during the raisin-bread cycle, or five minutes before the final kneading is finished.

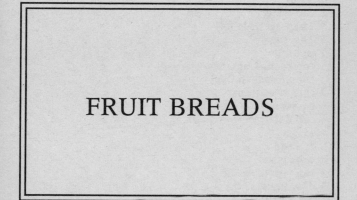

FRUIT BREADS

APPLE CINNAMON RAISIN BREAD

A very nice loaf with a wonderful, moist texture.

1 lb. Loaf
  1 cup water
  2 Tbs. vegetable oil
  3 Tbs. molasses
  ¾ tsp. salt
  1 tsp. cinnamon
  ½ cup whole-wheat flour
  ½ cup oatmeal
  2 cups bread flour
1½ tsp. yeast
  ½ cup diced apple
  ½ cup raisins

1½ lb. Loaf
1⅓ cups water
  3 Tbs. vegetable oil
  ¼ cup molasses
  1 tsp. salt
1½ tsp. cinnamon
  ⅔ cup whole-wheat flour
  ⅔ cup oatmeal
2⅔ cups bread flour
2½ tsp. yeast
  ¾ cup diced apple
  ⅔ cup raisins

Bake according to manufacturer's instructions, adding the raisins and apple during the raisin-bread cycle, or five minutes before the final kneading is finished.

CASHEW BANANA BREAD

This moist bread is wonderful eaten warm with honey. You can buy cashew butter at specialty food shops and health-food stores; or make your own by grinding one cup unsalted cashews in a blender or food processor with a drizzle of vegetable oil until it becomes smooth.

1 lb. Loaf
    1 cup mashed banana
    1 egg
 ½ cup cashew butter
    1 Tbs. vegetable oil
 ¼ cup honey
    1 tsp. salt
1½ cups whole-wheat flour
1½ cups bread flour
1½ tsp. yeast
 ½ cup cashews, chopped

1½ lb. Loaf
1¼ cups mashed banana
1½ eggs
 ⅔ cup cashew butter
1½ Tbs. vegetable oil
 ⅓ cup honey
1½ tsp. salt
    2 cups whole-wheat flour
    2 cups bread flour
2½ tsp. yeast
 ⅔ cup cashews, chopped

Bake according to manufacturer's instructions, adding the cashews during the raisin-bread cycle, or five minutes before the final kneading is finished.

BUCKWHEAT BANANA BREAD

A dark, hearty, none-too-sweet loaf with a strong buckwheat flavor. Good for breakfast.

1 lb. Loaf
  ½ cup buttermilk
  1 small banana, sliced
  3 Tbs. vegetable oil
  3 Tbs. honey
  ¾ tsp. vanilla extract
  1 tsp. salt
  ½ cup buckwheat flour
  2½ cups bread flour
  1½ tsp. yeast

1½ lb. Loaf
  ⅔ cup buttermilk
  1 large banana, sliced
  ¼ cup vegetable oil
  ¼ cup honey
  1 tsp. vanilla extract
  1⅓ tsp. salt
  ⅔ cup buckwheat flour
  3⅓ cups bread flour
  2½ tsp. yeast

Bake according to manufacturer's instructions.

CINNAMON BANANA OAT BREAD

Another wonderful breakfast bread which also makes great cream cheese sandwiches.

1 lb. Loaf
   1 cup mashed banana
   1 egg
   2 Tbs. vegetable oil
   3 Tbs. molasses
   1 tsp. salt
   1 tsp. cinnamon
   ¾ cup oatmeal
   ¾ cup whole-wheat flour
1½ cups bread flour
1½ tsp. yeast

1½ lb. Loaf
1¼ cups mashed banana
1½ eggs
   3 Tbs. vegetable oil
   ¼ cup molasses
1½ tsp. salt
1⅓ tsp. cinnamon
   1 cup oatmeal
   1 cup whole-wheat flour
   2 cups bread flour
2½ tsp. yeast

Bake according to manufacturer's instructions.

BLUEBERRY BRAN BREAD

Frozen blueberries work very well in this recipe, and are available all year round. Just thaw and drain them well before measuring.

1 lb. Loaf
 ⅔ cup buttermilk
 2 Tbs. butter
 2 Tbs. honey
 ¾ cup blueberries
1½ tsp. salt
 ½ cup bran
 ½ cup whole-wheat flour
 2 cups bread flour
1½ tsp. yeast

1½ lb. Loaf
 1 cup buttermilk
 3 Tbs. butter
 3 Tbs. honey
 1 cup blueberries
 2 tsp. salt
 ⅔ cup bran
 ⅔ cup whole-wheat flour
2⅔ cups bread flour
2½ tsp. yeast

Bake according to manufacturer's instructions.

BLUEBERRY CORN BREAD

Violet streaks in the deep yellow crumb, this beautiful bread is just as lovely to eat as it is to behold. Frozen blueberries work nicely—just thaw and drain them well.

1 lb. Loaf
- ¾ cup milk
- 3 Tbs. butter
- 2 eggs
- 3 Tbs. sugar
- 1 tsp. salt
- 1 cup cornmeal
- 2 cups bread flour
- 1½ tsp. yeast
- ½ cup blueberries

1½ lb. Loaf
- 1 cup milk
- 4 Tbs. butter
- 2½ eggs
- ¼ cup sugar
- 1½ tsp. salt
- 1½ cups cornmeal
- 2½ cups bread flour
- 2½ tsp. yeast
- ⅔ cup blueberries

Bake according to manufacturer's instructions, adding the blueberries during the raisin-bread cycle, or five minutes before the final kneading is finished.

CHERRY ALMOND BREAD

I am embarrassed to admit it, but I got the idea for this loaf from my hair conditioner. Despite this, it is a classic, wonderful combination. Find dried sour cherries at specialty food shops and by mail from American Spoon Foods (see sources listing, page 198).

1 lb. Loaf
1 cup milk
1 Tbs. butter
1 Tbs. almond paste
⅛ tsp. almond extract
2 Tbs. sugar
1 tsp. salt
½ cup whole-wheat flour
2 cups bread flour
1½ tsp. yeast
⅓ cup dried sour cherries
⅓ cup almonds, chopped

1½ lb. Loaf
1¼ cups milk
1½ Tbs. butter
1½ Tbs. almond paste
¼ tsp. almond extract
3 Tbs. sugar
1½ tsp. salt
⅔ cups whole-wheat flour
2⅓ cups bread flour
2½ tsp. yeast
½ cup dried sour cherries
½ cup almonds, chopped

Bake according to manufacturer's instructions, adding the cherries and almonds during the raisin-bread cycle, or five minutes before the final kneading is finished.

CRANBERRY BROWN BREAD

Bursting with tart cranberries, this satisfying bread is very beautiful when sliced—deep red fruit against a rich brown crumb.

1 lb. Loaf
    1 cup water
    3 Tbs. vegetable oil
    3 Tbs. molasses
    ¾ tsp. salt
    ½ tsp. cinnamon
    ½ tsp. ginger
    ⅛ tsp. powdered cloves
    ¼ cup wheat germ
    ¼ cup cornmeal
    ½ cup whole-wheat flour
    ½ cup oatmeal
    1½ cups bread flour
    2 Tbs. nonfat dry milk powder
    2 tsp. yeast
    ½ cup cranberries

1½ lb. Loaf
    1⅓ cups water
    ¼ cup vegetable oil
    ¼ cup molasses
    1 tsp. salt
    ¾ tsp. cinnamon
    ¾ tsp. ginger
    ¼ tsp. powdered cloves
    ⅓ cup wheat germ
    ⅓ cup cornmeal
    ⅔ cup whole-wheat flour
    ⅔ cup oatmeal
    2 cups bread flour
    3 Tbs. nonfat dry milk powder
    2½ tsp. yeast
    ¾ cup cranberries

Bake according to manufacturer's instructions, adding the cranberries during the raisin-bread cycle, or five minutes before the final kneading is finished.

HOT DATE BREAD

Sweet and peppery, this unusual bread is more than just interesting; it is delectable.

1 lb. Loaf

    1 cup yogurt
    1½ Tbs. vegetable oil
    1 Tbs. honey
    1 tsp. salt
    ½–1 tsp. cayenne pepper, to taste
    1 cup whole-wheat flour
    1½ cups bread flour
    2 Tbs. nonfat dry milk powder
    1½ tsp. yeast
    ⅓ cup dates, chopped

1½ lb. Loaf

    1⅓ cups yogurt
    2 Tbs. vegetable oil
    1½ Tbs. honey
    1½ tsp. salt
    ⅔–1¼ tsp. cayenne pepper, to taste
    1⅓ cups whole-wheat flour
    2 cups bread flour
    3 Tbs. nonfat dry milk powder
    2½ tsp. yeast
    ½ cup dates, chopped

Bake according to manufacturer's instructions, adding the dates during the raisin-bread cycle, or five minutes before the final kneading is finished.

FRUITED OAT BRAN BREAD

A nice, fruity oat bran bread that is light and moist. Its texture reminds me of a muffin, and I love it for breakfast or as a midafternoon snack. Feel free to alter the combination of fruits as the seasons and your moods change. Berries are especially nice in the summertime.

1 lb. Loaf
    1 cup water
    2 Tbs. vegetable oil
    2 Tbs. molasses
    1 tsp. salt
    ½ tsp. cinnamon
    1 cup oat bran
    ¾ cup whole-wheat flour
    1½ cups bread flour
    ¼ cup nonfat dry milk powder
    1 Tbs. gluten
    1½ tsp. yeast
    ¼ cup pear, diced
    ¼ cup raisins
    ¼ cup dried apricots, chopped

1½ lb. Loaf
    1⅓ cups water
    3 Tbs. vegetable oil
    3 Tbs. molasses
    1½ tsp. salt
    ⅔ tsp. cinnamon
    1⅓ cups oat bran
    1 cup whole-wheat flour
    1⅔ cups bread flour
    ⅓ cup nonfat dry milk powder
    1½ Tbs. gluten
    2½ tsp. yeast
    ⅓ cup pear, diced
    ⅓ cup raisins
    ⅓ cup dried apricots, chopped

Bake according to manufacturer's instructions, adding the fruit during the raisin-bread cycle, or five minutes before the final kneading is finished.

MANGO HONEY BREAD

This beautifully risen loaf has a subtle mango flavor, and is excellent served with chicken salad in the summertime.

1 lb. Loaf
 ¾ cup mango nectar
 2 Tbs. butter
 1 egg
 2 Tbs. honey
 1 tsp. salt
 3 cups bread flour
1½ tsp. yeast

1½ lb. Loaf
 1 cup mango nectar
 3 Tbs. butter
1½ eggs
 3 Tbs. honey
1½ tsp. salt
 4 cups bread flour
2½ tsp. yeast

Bake according to manufacturer's instructions.

ORANGE WHEAT BREAD

Both chopped orange sections and orange juice make for the sunny flavor of this bread.

1 lb. Loaf
1 cup orange juice
2 Tbs. butter
3 Tbs. molasses
1 tsp. salt
1 cup whole-wheat flour
1½ cups bread flour
3 Tbs. nonfat dry milk powder
1½ tsp. yeast
⅔ cup orange segments, chopped

1½ lb. Loaf
1¼ cups orange juice
3 Tbs. butter
¼ cup molasses
1½ tsp. salt
1⅓ cups whole-wheat flour
1⅔ cups bread flour
¼ cup nonfat dry milk powder
2½ tsp. yeast
¾ cup orange segments, chopped

Bake according to manufacturer's instructions, adding the orange segments during the raisin-bread cycle, or five minutes before the final kneading period is finished.

OATMEAL PEAR BREAD

A terrific, healthy loaf that is not too sweet. If you cannot find pear nectar, use milk. Also, if your dried pears feel tough and leathery, soak them in boiling water for fifteen minutes or so; they will plump right up.

1 lb. Loaf
- 1 cup pear nectar
- 2 Tbs. vegetable oil
- 2 Tbs. honey
- ¾ tsp. salt
- ½ cup whole-wheat flour
- 1 cup oatmeal
- 1½ cups bread flour
- 1½ tsp. yeast
- ½ cup dried pears, diced

1½ lb. Loaf
- 1⅓ cups pear nectar
- 3 Tbs. vegetable oil
- 3 Tbs. honey
- 1 tsp. salt
- ¾ cup whole-wheat flour
- 1¼ cups oatmeal
- 2 cups bread flour
- 2½ tsp. yeast
- ¾ cup dried pear, diced

Bake according to manufacturer's instructions, adding the pear during the raisin-bread cycle, or five minutes before the final kneading is finished.

CHAMOMILE RAISIN BREAD

This subtle, flowery bread has a honeylike flavor and an even, open crumb.

1 lb. Loaf
⅔ cup chamomile tea, brewed strong
½ cup golden raisins
1½ eggs
2 Tbs. butter
3 Tbs. sugar
½ tsp. salt
¾ cup whole-wheat flour
1½ cups bread flour
1½ tsp. yeast

1½ lb. Loaf
¾ cup chamomile tea, brewed strong
⅔ cup golden raisins
2 eggs
2½ Tbs. butter
¼ cup sugar
¾ tsp. salt
1 cup whole-wheat flour
2 cups bread flour
2½ tsp. yeast

Soak the raisins in the tea for at least one hour. Drain the raisins and add the tea to the bread. Add the rest of the ingredients except for the raisins. Bake according to manufacturer's instructions, adding the reserved raisins during the raisin-bread cycle, or five minutes before the final kneading is finished.

CINNAMON RAISIN BREAD

One of my favorite standards, I often serve this bread for brunch with orange butter and omelets. Everyone always wants the recipe.

1 lb. Loaf
- ¾ cup milk
- 1 egg
- 3 Tbs. butter
- 3 Tbs. honey
- 1 tsp. cinnamon
- 1 tsp. salt
- 3 cups bread flour
- 1½ tsp. yeast
- ½ cup raisins

1½ lb. Loaf
- 1 cup milk
- 1½ eggs
- 4 Tbs. butter
- ¼ cup honey
- 1½ tsp. cinnamon
- 1⅓ tsp. salt
- 3½ cups bread flour
- 2½ tsp. yeast
- ⅔ cup raisins

Bake according to manufacturer's instructions, adding the raisins during the raisin-bread cycle, or five minutes before the final kneading is finished.

EARL GREY TEA PRUNE BREAD

This is a high-rising, succulent loaf with plump prunes strewn throughout. The Earl Grey tea adds a subtle smoky background to the sweet fruit, and should be brewed doubly strong. I use two tea bags to make my cup.

1 lb. Loaf
- ⅔ cup Earl Grey tea, brewed strong
- 1½ eggs
- 2 Tbs. butter
- 3 Tbs. sugar
- ½ tsp. salt
- ¾ cup oatmeal
- 1½ cups bread flour
- 1½ tsp. yeast
- ½ cup pitted prunes, chopped

1½ lb. Loaf
- ¾ cup Earl Grey tea, brewed strong
- 2 eggs
- 2½ Tbs. butter
- ¼ cup sugar
- ¾ tsp. salt
- 1 cup oatmeal
- 2 cups bread flour
- 2½ tsp. yeast
- ⅔ cup pitted prunes, chopped

Soak the prunes in the tea for at least one hour. Drain the prunes and add the tea to the bread. Add the rest of the ingredients except for the prunes. Bake according to manufacturer's instructions, adding the reserved prunes during the raisin-bread cycle, or five minutes before the final kneading is finished.

PECAN PUMPKIN BREAD

Although I originally made this as a tasty pumpkin addition to my Thanksgiving table, I seem to get requests for it all year round!

1 lb. Loaf
- ¾ cup milk
- ⅔ cup pumpkin puree
- 2 Tbs. butter
- ¼ cup honey
- 1 tsp. cinnamon
- ¼ tsp. ground cloves
- 1 tsp. salt
- ½ cup whole-wheat flour
- 2½ cups bread flour
- 1½ tsp. yeast
- ¾ cup pecans, coarsely chopped

1½ lb. Loaf
- 1 cup milk
- ¾ cup pumpkin puree
- 3 Tbs. butter
- ⅓ cup honey
- 1⅓ tsp. cinnamon
- ⅓ tsp. ground cloves
- 1½ tsp. salt
- ¾ cup whole-wheat flour
- 3¼ cups bread flour
- 2½ tsp. yeast
- 1 cup pecans, coarsely chopped

Bake according to manufacturer's instructions, adding the pecans during the raisin-bread cycle, or five minutes before the final kneading is finished.

GINGERED RHUBARB BREAD

This bread rises magnificently and crowns the top of the bread pan with a golden toque. Although the heat from baking changes the dough's bright pink hue to a more subdued beige, its sprightly flavor more than makes up for the dull color.

1 lb. Loaf
1¼ cups stewed rhubarb
1½ Tbs. butter
2 Tbs. sugar
1 egg
½ tsp. salt
1 tsp. ginger
1 cup whole-wheat flour
2 cups bread flour
1½ tsp. yeast

1½ lb. Loaf
2 cups stewed rhubarb
2 Tbs. butter
2 Tbs. sugar
1½ eggs
⅔ tsp. salt
1½ tsp. ginger
1½ cups whole-wheat flour
2½ cups bread flour
2½ tsp. yeast

Bake according to manufacturer's instructions.

To make stewed rhubarb:
2 lbs. rhubarb stalks, washed and cubed
1–1½ cups sugar to taste
½ cup water or orange juice

Combine sugar, water or orange juice, and rhubarb in a saucepan over low heat. Simmer until the rhubarb falls apart and the sauce is thick, somewhat like a puree.

This is also excellent over vanilla ice cream.

STRAWBERRY CREAM CHEESE BREAD

The strawberries in this bread are subtle, but combine wonderfully with the cream cheese for a soft, light loaf.

1 lb. Loaf
- ⅓ cup milk
- ⅓ cup mashed strawberries
- ⅓ cup cream cheese
- 1 Tbs. butter
- 2 Tbs. honey
- 1 tsp. salt
- ½ cup oatmeal
- 1½ cups bread flour
- 1½ tsp. yeast

1½ lb. Loaf
- ½ cup milk
- ½ cup mashed strawberries
- ½ cup cream cheese
- 2 Tbs. butter
- 3 Tbs. honey
- 1⅓ tsp. salt
- 1 cup oatmeal
- 2 cups bread flour
- 2½ tsp. yeast

Bake according to manufacturer's instructions.

NUTMEG SWEET POTATO BREAD

This sweet bread is just the thing for autumn dinners. Serve it warm and slather it with good butter; it is a feast in itself.

1 lb. Loaf
- ⅓ cup milk
- 3 Tbs. butter
- ⅔ cup cooked sweet potato
- 3 Tbs. molasses
- ¾ tsp. freshly grated nutmeg
- 2 Tbs. sugar
- 1 tsp. salt
- ½ cup whole-wheat flour
- 1½ cups bread flour
- 1½ tsp. yeast

1½ lb. Loaf
- ½ cup milk
- 4 Tbs. butter
- 1 cup cooked sweet potato
- ¼ cup molasses
- 1 tsp. freshly grated nutmeg
- 3 Tbs. sugar
- 1½ tsp. salt
- 1 cup whole-wheat flour
- 2 cups bread flour
- 2½ tsp. yeast

Bake according to manufacturer's instructions.

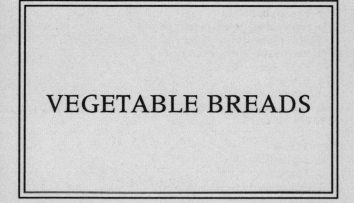

VEGETABLE BREADS

AVOCADO CORN BREAD

Avocado gives this bread a moist and chewy texture and a marvelously subtle flavor. Because of the natural oils found in avocados, I was able to cut down on the added fat. Use only California (Haas) avocados, which when ripe have a black, nubby skin. This bread makes super sandwiches.

1 lb. Loaf
1 cup water
1 small avocado, mashed
2 Tbs. olive oil
1 egg
1 tsp. pepper
2 tsp. sugar
1 tsp. salt
1 cup cornmeal
2 cups bread flour
1½ tsp. yeast

1½ lb. Loaf
1⅓ cups water
1 large avocado, mashed
3 Tbs. olive oil
1½ eggs
1½ tsp. pepper
1 Tbs. sugar
1⅓ tsp. salt
1⅓ cups cornmeal
2⅔ cups bread flour
2½ tsp. yeast

Bake according to manufacturer's instructions.

BORSCHT BREAD

Otherwise known as "think pink" bread, this is a stunning, rose-colored loaf that is just the thing when you need pink bread (if you never need pink bread, make it anyway because it tastes great). Two of my tasters devoured it in one sitting—less than ten minutes flat.

1 lb. Loaf
- ¾ cup cooked, sliced beets
- ⅔ cup sour cream
- 2 Tbs. butter
- 2 tsp. sugar
- 1 tsp. salt
- ¼ cup fresh dill
- 2½ cups bread flour
- 1½ tsp. yeast

1½ lb. Loaf
- 1 cup cooked, sliced beets
- ¾ cup sour cream
- 3 Tbs. butter
- 1 Tbs. sugar
- 1½ tsp. salt
- ⅓ cup fresh dill
- 3⅓ cups bread flour
- 2½ tsp. yeast

Bake according to manufacturer's instructions.

BROCCOLI CHEDDAR BREAD

This bread, served warm, is a tasty hors d'oeuvre. You may substitute any other kind of cheese for the cheddar; Swiss and smoked gouda are especially nice changes.

1 lb. Loaf
 ⅔ cup buttermilk
 1½ Tbs. olive oil
 1 egg
   Dash of Tabasco
 ½ tsp. sugar
 1 tsp. salt
 ⅔ tsp. pepper
 ¼ cup onions, chopped
 2⅔ cups bread flour
 1½ tsp. yeast
 ⅔ cup steamed broccoli florets, chopped
 ⅔ cup cheddar cheese, grated

1½ lb. Loaf
 ¾ cup buttermilk
 2 Tbs. olive oil
 1½ eggs
   Dash of Tabasco
 ¾ tsp. sugar
 1½ tsp. salt
 1 tsp. pepper
 ⅓ cup onions, chopped
 3¼ cups bread flour
 2½ tsp. yeast
 ¾ cup steamed broccoli florets, chopped
 ¾ cup cheddar cheese, grated

Bake according to manufacturer's instructions, adding the broccoli and cheddar during the raisin-bread cycle, or five minutes before the final kneading is finished.

OVERKILL HEALTH BREAD
(Oat bran broccoli bread)

I made up this recipe as a joke, but it turned out to be as tasty as it is healthy. Try making a hummus sandwich with slices of this chewy bread.

1 lb. Loaf
- ¾ cup water
- ½ cup cooked broccoli florets, chopped
- ⅓ cup cottage cheese
- 1½ Tbs. vegetable oil
- 1 Tbs. molasses
- 1 tsp. salt
- 1 cup oat bran
- ¾ cup whole-wheat flour
- 1½ cups bread flour
- ¼ cup nonfat dry milk powder
- 1 Tbs. gluten
- 1½ tsp. yeast

1½ lb. Loaf
- 1 cup water
- ⅔ cup cooked broccoli florets, chopped
- ½ cup cottage cheese
- 2 Tbs. vegetable oil
- 2 Tbs. molasses
- 1½ tsp. salt
- 1⅓ cups oat bran
- 1 cup whole-wheat flour
- 1⅔ cups bread flour
- ⅓ cup nonfat dry milk powder
- 1½ Tbs. gluten
- 2½ tsp. yeast

Bake according to manufacturer's instructions.

EGGPLANT CILANTRO BREAD

An unusual savory loaf best made in late summer when ripe, purple eggplants are stacked high at farmers' markets.

1 lb. Loaf
- ¼ cup water
- 2 Tbs. olive oil
- 1 cup cooked eggplant, mashed
  Dash of Tabasco
- ⅓ cup cilantro
- 1 clove garlic, chopped
- 1 tsp. sugar
- ½ tsp. pepper
- 1 tsp. salt
- ½ cup whole-wheat flour
- 2 cups bread flour
- 2 tsp. yeast

1½ lb. Loaf
- ⅓ cup water
- 3 Tbs. olive oil
- 1¼ cups cooked eggplant, mashed
  Dash of Tabasco
- ½ cup cilantro
- 1½ cloves of garlic, chopped
- 1½ tsp. sugar
- ¾ tsp. pepper
- 1½ tsp. salt
- ¾ cup whole-wheat flour
- 2½ cups bread flour
- 1 Tbs. yeast

Bake according to manufacturer's instructions.

RED ONION–CAPER BREAD

Red onions are sweeter than regular onions, and together with the capers make for a most succulent bread.

1 lb. Loaf
    1 cup water
1½ Tbs. vegetable oil
    1 Tbs. honey
  ½ tsp. pepper
    1 tsp. salt
    1 cup whole-wheat flour
1½ cups bread flour
    2 Tbs. nonfat dry milk powder
1½ tsp. yeast
  ⅓ cup red onion, chopped
  ¼ cup capers

1½ lb. Loaf
1⅓ cups water
    2 Tbs. vegetable oil
1½ Tbs. honey
  ⅔ tsp. pepper
1½ tsp. salt
1⅓ cups whole-wheat flour
    2 cups bread flour
    3 Tbs. nonfat dry milk powder
2½ tsp. yeast
  ½ cup red onion, chopped
  ⅓ cup capers

Bake according to manufacturer's instructions, adding the onion and capers during the raisin-bread cycle, or five minutes before the final kneading is finished.

POTATO LEEK BREAD

A tantalizing twist on this classic combination; serve it at your most special occasions.

1 lb. Loaf
  ½ cup milk
  3 Tbs. butter
  1 egg
  ⅓ cup mashed potatoes
  1 Tbs. sugar
  1 tsp. salt
  ¼ tsp. freshly grated nutmeg
  2 cups bread flour
1½ tsp. yeast
  ⅔ cup sautéed leeks

1½ lb. Loaf
  ¾ cup milk
  4 Tbs. butter
1½ eggs
  ½ cup mashed potatoes
1½ Tbs. sugar
1½ tsp. salt
  ⅓ tsp. freshly grated nutmeg
  3 cups bread flour
2½ tsp. yeast
  ¾ cup sautéed leeks

Bake according to manufacturer's instructions, adding the leeks during the raisin-bread cycle, or five minutes before the final kneading is finished.

RED PEPPER CORN BREAD

A robust, high-rising loaf with an open, moist crumb. I love it with salad for a light dinner.

1 lb. Loaf
1 cup milk
¼ cup olive oil
1 egg
1 tsp. pepper
2 tsp. sugar
1 tsp. salt
1 cup cornmeal
2 cups bread flour
1½ tsp. yeast
1 cup red pepper, chopped

1½ lb. Loaf
1⅓ cups milk
⅓ cup olive oil
1½ eggs
1⅓ tsp. pepper
1 Tbs. sugar
1⅓ tsp. salt
1⅓ cups cornmeal
2⅔ cups bread flour
2½ tsp. yeast
1⅓ cups red pepper, chopped

Bake according to manufacturer's instructions, adding the red pepper during the raisin-bread cycle, or five minutes before the final kneading is finished.

SPINACH ONION CORN BREAD

Spinach is one of those vegetables I always keep on hand in the freezer. That way I can whip up this loaf anytime someone asks for it (which is pretty often). Don't be put off by the bread's weird color—its flavor more than compensates for its flush.

1 lb. Loaf
- ½ cup buttermilk
- 2 Tbs. olive oil
- 1 tsp. sugar
- 1 cup cooked spinach, well drained
- ⅓ cup onion, chopped
- ½ tsp. pepper
- 1 tsp. salt
- ¼ cup whole-wheat flour
- ½ cup cornmeal
- 1¼ cups bread flour
- 2 Tbs. nonfat dry milk powder
- 1½ tsp. yeast

1½ lb. Loaf
- ⅔ cup buttermilk
- 2½ Tbs. olive oil
- 2 tsp. sugar
- 1¼ cups cooked spinach, well drained
- ½ cup onion, chopped
- ⅔ tsp. pepper
- 1½ tsp. salt
- ⅓ cup whole-wheat flour
- ⅔ cup cornmeal
- 2 cups bread flour
- 3 Tbs. nonfat dry milk powder
- 2½ tsp. yeast

Bake according to manufacturer's instructions.

WATERCRESS PEA BREAD

This pretty green loaf has a bright, fresh fragrance—like that of a cool spring evening.

1 lb. Loaf
¼ cup sour cream
1⅓ cups cottage cheese
2 Tbs. butter
2 eggs
½ cup watercress, chopped
1 Tbs. sugar
1 tsp. salt
2½ cups bread flour
1½ tsp. yeast
½ cup green peas, cooked

1½ lb. Loaf
⅓ cup sour cream
1½ cups cottage cheese
2½ Tbs. butter
2½ eggs
⅔ cup watercress, chopped
1½ Tbs. sugar
1½ tsp. salt
3 cups bread flour
2½ tsp. yeast
⅔ cup green peas, cooked

Bake according to manufacturer's instructions, adding the peas during the raisin-bread cycle, or five minutes before the final kneading is finished.

YOGURT CARROT BREAD

A gorgeous, pale orange loaf that slices terrifically. It is my favorite bread for tunafish salad.

1 lb. Loaf
- ½ cup plain yogurt
- 2 Tbs. butter
- 1 Tbs. honey
- 1 cup grated carrots
- ⅓ cup fresh parsley
- ½ tsp. pepper
- 1 tsp. salt
- ¼ cup whole-wheat flour
- 1¾ cups bread flour
- 2 Tbs. nonfat dry milk powder
- 1½ tsp. yeast

1½ lb. Loaf
- ⅔ cup plain yogurt
- 2½ Tbs. butter
- 1½ Tbs. honey
- 1¼ cups grated carrots
- ½ cup fresh parsley
- ⅔ tsp. pepper
- 1½ tsp. salt
- ½ cup whole-wheat flour
- 2 cups bread flour
- 3 Tbs. nonfat dry milk powder
- 2½ tsp. yeast

Bake according to manufacturer's instructions.

ZUCCHINI PARMESAN BREAD

A healthy loaf that's just the thing in the late summer when neighborhood gardeners try and foist their abundant zucchini on you.

1 lb. Loaf
- ¼ cup buttermilk
- 1 egg
- 1 Tbs. butter
- 1 cup zucchini, diced
- ¼ cup fresh parsley
- 1 Tbs. honey
- 1 tsp. salt
- ½ tsp. pepper
- 2 Tbs. Parmesan cheese, grated
- ¼ cup bulgur
- ½ cup whole-wheat flour
- 1½ cups bread flour
- 1½ tsp. yeast

1½ lb. Loaf
- ⅓ cup buttermilk
- 1½ eggs
- 1½ Tbs. butter
- 1½ cups zucchini, diced
- ⅓ cup fresh parsley
- 1½ Tbs. honey
- 2 tsp. salt
- ⅔ tsp. pepper
- 3 Tbs. Parmesan cheese, grated
- ⅓ cup bulgur
- ⅔ cup whole-wheat flour
- 2¼ cups bread flour
- 2½ tsp. yeast

Bake according to manufacturer's instructions.

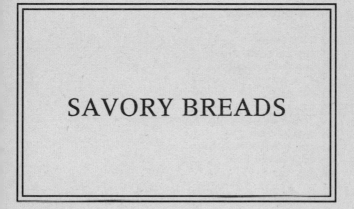

SAVORY BREADS

BAGEL BREAD

Although the bread machine cannot, by itself, make a bagel-textured bread, by putting my favorite bagel toppings into the dough, I can at least approximate the **flavor** of a chewy New York bagel. Serve this one with smoked salmon and cream cheese for brunch if you cannot get good bagels nearby.

1 lb. Loaf
- 1 cup water
- 1 Tbs. vegetable oil
- 1 Tbs. sugar
- 1½ tsp. salt
- 1 tsp. poppy seeds
- 1 tsp. sesame seeds
- 2 cups bread flour
- 1½ tsp. yeast
- 3 Tbs. sautéed onions

1½ lb. Loaf
- 1½ cups water
- 1½ Tbs. vegetable oil
- 1½ Tbs. sugar
- 2 tsp. salt
- 1½ tsp. poppy seeds
- 1½ tsp. sesame seeds
- 3 cups bread flour
- 2½ tsp. yeast
- ¼ cup sautéed onions

Bake according to manufacturer's instructions, adding the onions during the raisin-bread cycle, or five minutes before the final kneading is finished.

CUMIN BREAD

This mildly spiced bread is perfect to serve with an Indian curry.

1 lb. Loaf
- 1 cup cottage cheese
- 2 eggs
- 2 Tbs. honey
- 1 clove garlic, mashed
- 1½ Tbs. cumin seeds
- 1 tsp. salt
- ¼ tsp. baking soda
- 2½ cups bread flour
- 1½ tsp. yeast

1½ lb. Loaf
- 1⅓ cups cottage cheese
- 2½ eggs
- 3 Tbs. honey
- 1½ cloves garlic, chopped
- 2 Tbs. cumin seeds
- 1⅓ tsp. salt
- ⅓ tsp. baking soda
- 3⅓ cups bread flour
- 2½ tsp. yeast

Bake according to manufacturer's instructions.

DOUBLE DILL BREAD

Fresh dill and dill seeds each contribute a slightly different flavor to this moist, well-risen bread.

1 lb. Loaf
  1 cup plain yogurt
  ½ cup cottage cheese
  2 Tbs. butter
  1 egg
  2 tsp. sugar
  ¼ cup fresh dill
  ¾ tsp. dill seeds
  1 tsp. salt
  ½ cup whole-wheat flour
  2 cups bread flour
  1½ tsp. yeast

1½ lb. Loaf
  1¼ cups plain yogurt
  ⅔ cup cottage cheese
  2½ Tbs. butter
  1½ eggs
  1 Tbs. sugar
  ⅓ cup fresh dill
  1 tsp. dill seeds
  1½ tsp. salt
  ⅔ cup whole-wheat flour
  2⅔ cups bread flour
  2½ tsp. yeast

Bake according to manufacturer's instructions.

HERBED RICOTTA BREAD

Tender and light, this is a wonderful summery bread. Feel free to alter the combination of herbs to your taste; this loaf takes very well to substitutions.

1 lb. Loaf
¼ cup milk
1⅓ cups ricotta cheese
2 Tbs. butter
2 eggs
3 Tbs. fresh oregano
2 Tbs. parsley
3 Tbs. fresh basil
2 Tbs. fresh thyme
1 Tbs. sugar
1 tsp. salt
2½ cups bread flour
1½ tsp. yeast

1½ lb. Loaf
⅓ cup milk
1½ cups ricotta cheese
2½ Tbs. butter
2½ eggs
4 Tbs. fresh oregano
2½ Tbs. parsley
4 Tbs. fresh basil
2½ Tbs. fresh thyme
1½ Tbs. sugar
1½ tsp. salt
3 cups bread flour
2½ tsp. yeast

Bake according to manufacturer's instructions.

GARLIC PARMESAN BREAD

I first made this bread to use as croutons in a Caesar salad. It has all the flavor of regular croutons sautéed in oil and garlic, but not nearly as much fat. Simply dry out cubes of it in a slow oven (250 degrees) and toss with your lettuce and dressing. Or eat it as is with any Italian meal. It is excellent.

1 lb. Loaf
- ½ cup milk
- 1 cup ricotta cheese
- ¼ cup Parmesan cheese, grated
- 2 Tbs. olive oil
- 2–3 cloves of garlic, smashed
- 2 tsp. freshly ground black pepper
- 1 tsp. sugar
- 1 tsp. salt
- 2½ cups bread flour
- 1½ tsp. yeast

1½ lb. Loaf
- ⅔ cup milk
- 1¼ cups ricotta cheese
- ⅓ cup Parmesan cheese, grated
- 2½ Tbs. olive oil
- 3–5 cloves of garlic, smashed
- 1 Tbs. freshly ground black pepper
- 2 tsp. sugar
- 1½ tsp. salt
- 3 cups bread flour
- 2½ tsp. yeast

Bake according to manufacturer's instructions.

FRESH JALAPEÑO CORN BREAD

Fiery hot, this bread is best made with fresh jalapeño peppers. Canned, pickled peppers are good in a pinch, but you may want to increase the amount since pickling them can decrease their heat. Furthermore, the heat of any pepper is carried in the little white seeds attached to the inner membranes. If you prefer your bread to be less hot, simply scrape away the majority of those seeds. Remember always to wear rubber gloves when handling hot peppers, or they could burn your skin.

1 lb. Loaf
- 1 cup water
- 1–2 chopped fresh jalapeño peppers, to taste
- ¼ cup olive oil
- 1 egg
- 1 tsp. pepper
- 2 tsp. sugar
- 1 tsp. salt
- 1 cup cornmeal
- 2 cups bread flour
- 1½ tsp. yeast

1½ lb. Loaf
- 1⅓ cups milk
- 1½–2½ chopped fresh jalapeño peppers, to taste
- ⅓ cup olive oil
- 1½ eggs
- 1⅓ tsp. pepper
- 1 Tbs. sugar
- 1⅓ tsp. salt
- 1⅓ cups cornmeal
- 2⅔ cups bread flour
- 2½ tsp. yeast

Bake according to manufacturer's instructions.

SAVORY SPICY BREAD

A rich, aromatic bread that is perfect to serve with a vegetarian meal. Heating the saffron with the milk helps release all the flavor packed into those vibrant strands. It also produces a gorgeous bright orange color. Cumin seeds are easily toasted by placing them in a red-hot frying pan and shaking until the seeds begin to turn black, and the aroma fills the kitchen. This takes about three minutes.

1 lb. Loaf
- ½ cup milk
- ¼ tsp. saffron threads
- ½ cup plain yogurt
- 2 Tbs. vegetable oil
- 1 Tbs. honey
- 1 tsp. salt
- ¼ cup fresh cilantro leaves
- ¼–½ tsp. cayenne pepper, to taste
- ½ tsp. cardamom seeds, crushed
- ½ tsp. cumin seeds, toasted
- ½ tsp. coriander powder
- 1½ cups whole-wheat flour
- 1½ cups bread flour
- 1½ tsp. yeast

1½ lb. Loaf
- ⅔ cup milk
- ⅓ tsp. saffron threads
- ⅔ cup plain yogurt
- 3 Tbs. vegetable oil
- 1½ Tbs. honey
- 1½ tsp. salt
- ⅓ cup fresh cilantro leaves
- ⅓–⅔ tsp. cayenne pepper, to taste
- ⅔ tsp. cardamom seeds, crushed
- ⅔ tsp. cumin seeds, toasted
- ⅔ tsp. coriander powder
- 2 cups whole-wheat flour
- 2 cups bread flour
- 2½ tsp. yeast

Heat the milk and saffron in a saucepan until the milk is scalded (that is, until bubbles appear on the edges of the pan). Remove from heat and allow to cool until it feels barely warm to the touch.

Add to the bread pan with the other ingredients, and bake according to manufacturer's instructions.

HEARTY ONION STOUT BREAD

The stout in this recipe refers to the type of beer, not the shape of the loaf. Use the darkest stout you can find.

1 lb. Loaf
 ¾ **cup dark stout**
 2 **Tbs. vegetable oil**
 ¼ **cup onions, chopped**
 ⅓ **cup molasses**
 ½ **tsp. salt**
 1 **Tbs. caraway seeds**
 ½ **cup whole-wheat flour**
 ½ **cup rye flour**
 1¼ **cups bread flour**
 1½ **tsp. yeast**

1½ lb. Loaf
 1 **cup dark stout**
 2½ **Tbs. vegetable oil**
 ⅓ **cup onions, chopped**
 ⅓ **cup molasses**
 1 **tsp. salt**
 1½ **Tbs. caraway seeds**
 ⅔ **cup whole-wheat flour**
 ⅔ **cup rye flour**
 2½ **cups bread flour**
 2½ **tsp. yeast**

Bake according to manufacturer's instructions.

HOMINY BLACK PEPPER
CORN BREAD

The hominy in this excellent corn bread makes it very tender. Hominy is available in cans; just rinse the contents in fresh water before you add it to the machine.

1 lb. Loaf
1 cup water
¼ cup olive oil
1 egg
1 Tbs. freshly ground black pepper
2 tsp. sugar
1 tsp. salt
1 cup cornmeal
2 cups bread flour
1½ tsp. yeast
1½ cups hominy

1½ lb. Loaf
1⅓ cups water
⅓ cup olive oil
1½ eggs
1½ Tbs. freshly ground black pepper
1 Tbs. sugar
1⅓ tsp. salt
1⅓ cups cornmeal
2⅔ cups bread flour
2½ tsp. yeast
2 cups hominy

Bake according to manufacturer's instructions, adding the hominy during the raisin-bread cycle, or five minutes before the final kneading is finished.

OLIVE COUNTRY BREAD

This flaky, crusty bread is divine for picnics and other al fresco dining. Do use the lard if you are not watching your cholesterol too fanatically; it imparts a lovely, characteristic nuttiness that really sets this bread apart.

1 lb. Loaf
- 1 cup water
- 2 Tbs. fresh lard, or olive oil
- 2 tsp. sugar
- 1 tsp. salt
- 1 Tbs. dried rosemary or 3 Tbs. fresh
- 1½ cups whole-wheat flour
- 1½ cups bread flour
- 1½ tsp. yeast
- ⅔ cup pitted Moroccan olives, or other good-quality black olives

1½ lb. Loaf
- 1⅓ cups water
- 3 Tbs. fresh lard, or olive oil
- 1 Tbs. sugar
- 1½ tsp. salt
- 1½ Tbs. dried rosemary or ¼ cup fresh
- 2 cups whole-wheat flour
- 2 cups bread flour
- 2½ tsp. yeast
- ¾ cup pitted Moroccan olives, or other good quality black olives

Bake according to manufacturer's instructions, adding the olives during the raisin-bread cycle, or five minutes before the final kneading is finished.

CAPER OLIVE BREAD

This pungent bread is riddled with green flecks from the olives, parsley, and capers. Try it spread with fresh goat cheese and sliced ripe tomatoes as an appetizer or light meal.

1 lb. Loaf
  1 cup water
  2 Tbs. olive oil
  ⅓ cup fresh parsley
  2 tsp. sugar
  1 tsp. salt
1½ cups whole-wheat flour
1½ cups bread flour
1½ tsp. yeast
  ⅓ cup capers
  ⅓ cup pitted green olives

1½ lb. Loaf
1⅓ cups water
  3 Tbs. olive oil
  ½ cup fresh parsley
  1 Tbs. sugar
1½ tsp. salt
  2 cups whole-wheat flour
  2 cups bread flour
2½ tsp. yeast
  ½ cup capers
  ½ cup pitted green olives

Bake according to manufacturer's instructions, adding the olives and capers during the raisin-bread cycle, or five minutes before the final kneading is finished.

SUN-DRIED TOMATO HERB BREAD

A bright-tasting dense bread that is wonderful toasted and drizzled with extra-virgin olive oil.

1 lb. Loaf
  1 cup water
  2 Tbs. olive oil
  ¼ cup fresh basil leaves
  2 Tbs. fresh parsley leaves
  1 clove garlic, mashed
  2 tsp. sugar
  1 tsp. salt
  ¾ tsp. pepper
  1 cup whole-wheat flour
  2 cups bread flour
1½ tsp. yeast
  ½ cup oil-packed sun-dried tomatoes, chopped

1½ lb. Loaf
1⅓ cups water
  3 Tbs. olive oil
  ⅓ cup fresh basil leaves
  3 Tbs. fresh parsley leaves
1½ cloves garlic, mashed
2½ tsp. sugar
1½ tsp. salt
  1 tsp. pepper
1½ cups whole-wheat flour
2½ cups bread flour
2½ tsp. yeast
  ⅔ cup oil-packed sun-dried tomatoes, chopped

Bake according to manufacturer's instructions, adding the sun-dried tomatoes during the raisin-bread cycle, or five minutes before the final kneading is finished.

PROSCIUTTO OLIVE TOMATO BREAD

This meal-in-a-loaf is absolutely terrific with a salad and a bottle of red wine for a perfect summer lunch or light dinner. It has a pale rose cast to the crumb—a result of the purple olives and red tomatoes.

1 lb. Loaf
1 cup water
2 Tbs. vegetable oil
⅓ cup ripe tomato, chopped
⅓ cup pitted Alfonse, or other wine-cured olives
⅓ cup prosciutto, shredded
2 tsp. sugar
½ tsp. sage
1 tsp. salt
⅓ cup rye flour
1½ cups whole-wheat flour
1½ cups bread flour
1½ tsp. yeast

1½ lb. Loaf
1⅓ cups water
3 Tbs. vegetable oil
½ cup ripe tomato, chopped
½ cup pitted Alfonse, or other wine-cured olives
⅓ cup prosciutto, shredded
1 Tbs. sugar
⅔ tsp. sage
1½ tsp. salt
½ cup rye flour
1⅔ cups whole-wheat flour
2 cups bread flour
2½ tsp. yeast

Bake according to manufacturer's instructions.

CHESTNUT STUFFING BREAD

Since peeled whole chestnuts are available year round in large supermarkets, you needn't wait until autumn to serve this rich, zesty bread. Use either breakfast or Italian sausage.

1 lb. Loaf
  1 cup water
  2 Tbs. olive oil
  1 egg
  ½ cup cooked sausage, crumbled
  1 tsp. sugar
  ½ tsp. freshly grated nutmeg
  ⅓ tsp. celery seeds
  1 tsp. dried sage, or 1 Tbs. fresh
  ¼ cup fresh parsley
  1 tsp. salt
  ½ cup cornmeal
  ½ cup rye flour
1½ cups bread flour
1½ tsp. yeast
  ½ cup peeled chestnuts, chopped
  ¼ cup sautéed onions

1½ lb. Loaf
1¼ cups water
2½ Tbs. olive oil
1½ eggs
  ⅔ cup cooked sausage, crumbled
1½ tsp. sugar
  ⅔ tsp. freshly grated nutmeg
  ½ tsp. celery seeds
1¼ tsp. dried sage, or 1½ Tbs. fresh
  ⅓ cup fresh parsley
1½ tsp. salt
  ⅔ cup cornmeal
  ⅔ cup rye flour
  2 cups bread flour
2½ tsp. yeast
  ⅔ cup peeled chestnuts, chopped
  ⅓ cup sautéed onions

Bake according to manufacturer's instructions, adding the chestnuts and onion during the raisin-bread cycle, or five minutes before the final kneading is finished.

SMOKY BREAD

The smoke flavor in this bread comes from the bacon and smoked cheddar. It is an especially flavorful loaf.

1 lb. Loaf
- 1 cup water
- 1 egg
- 1½ Tbs. butter
- ⅔ cup smoked cheddar
- 2 tsp. sugar
- ½ tsp. pepper
- 1 tsp. salt
- 1 cup whole-wheat flour
- 1½ cups bread flour
- 2 Tbs. nonfat dry milk powder
- 1½ tsp. yeast
- ⅓ cup cooked bacon, crumbled

1½ lb. Loaf
- 1⅓ cups water
- 1½ eggs
- 2 Tbs. butter
- ¾ cup smoked cheddar
- 1 Tbs. sugar
- ⅔ tsp. pepper
- 1½ tsp. salt
- 1⅓ cups whole-wheat flour
- 2 cups bread flour
- 3 Tbs. nonfat dry milk powder
- 2½ tsp. yeast
- ½ cup cooked bacon, crumbled

Bake according to manufacturer's instructions, adding the bacon during the raisin-bread cycle, or five minutes before the final kneading is finished.

BLUE CHEESE–CELERY BREAD

The celery in this bread is refreshing next to the tangy blue cheese background. It is superb all by itself, although I imagine it would be wonderful with buffalo chicken wings.

1 lb. Loaf
½ cup milk
½ cup sour cream
1 egg
1½ Tbs. butter
⅔ cup blue cheese
¾ tsp. celery seeds
2 tsp. sugar
½ tsp. pepper
1 tsp. salt
1 cup whole-wheat flour
1½ cups bread flour
2 Tbs. nonfat dry milk powder
1½ tsp. yeast
⅓ cup celery, chopped

1½ lb. Loaf
⅔ cup milk
⅔ cup sour cream
1½ eggs
2 Tbs. butter
¾ cup blue cheese
1 tsp. celery seeds
1 Tbs. sugar
⅔ tsp. pepper
1½ tsp. salt
1⅓ cups whole-wheat flour
2 cups bread flour
3 Tbs. nonfat dry milk powder
2½ tsp. yeast
½ cup celery, chopped

Bake according to manufacturer's instructions, adding the celery during the raisin-bread cycle, or five minutes before the final kneading is finished.

THAI SATAY BREAD

I got the idea for this spicy bread from my friend Amy Martin, who has been known to eat the pungent peanut sauce served at Thai restaurants straight—with a spoon.

1 lb. Loaf
1 cup milk
1 Tbs. sesame oil
1 Tbs. olive oil
1 tsp. chile oil
1 Tbs. lemon juice
½ cup peanut butter
1 clove garlic, smashed
2 Tbs. onion, chopped
¼ cup fresh basil
2 tsp. soy sauce
⅓ tsp. salt
½ cup whole-wheat flour
2 cups bread flour
1½ tsp. yeast

1½ lb. Loaf
1⅓ cups milk
1½ Tbs. sesame oil
1½ Tbs. olive oil
1¼ tsp. chile oil
1½ Tbs. lemon juice
⅔ cup peanut butter
1½ cloves garlic, smashed
3 Tbs. onion, chopped
⅓ cup fresh basil
1 Tbs. soy sauce
½ tsp. salt
⅔ cup whole-wheat flour
2⅔ cups bread flour
2½ tsp. yeast

Bake according to manufacturer's instructions.

CHINESE BLACK BEAN SAUCE–
SCALLION BREAD

My passion for anything with black bean sauce led me to create this intensely flavored loaf. Sliced thin, toasted, spread with olive oil, and topped with fresh scallion, this makes a fantastic hors d'oeuvre. You can buy black bean sauce in the ethnic-food section of most supermarkets, not to mention in Chinese specialty markets.

1 lb. Loaf
- ¼ cup black bean sauce
- ¾ cup water
- 1 Tbs. cooking sherry
- 1½ Tbs. vegetable oil
- 1 tsp. sesame oil
- 2 tsp. sugar
- ½ tsp. salt
- 1 cup whole-wheat flour
- 1½ cups bread flour
- 2 Tbs. nonfat dry milk powder
- 1½ tsp. yeast
- ½ cup scallions, chopped

1½ lb. Loaf
- ⅓ cup black bean sauce
- 1 cup water
- 1½ Tbs. cooking sherry
- 2 Tbs. vegetable oil
- 2 tsp. sesame oil
- 1 Tbs. sugar
- ⅔ tsp. salt
- 1⅓ cups whole-wheat flour
- 2 cups bread flour
- 3 Tbs. nonfat dry milk powder
- 2½ tsp. yeast
- ⅔ cup scallions, chopped

Bake according to manufacturer's instructions, adding the scallions during the raisin-bread cycle, or five minutes before the final kneading is finished.

WHITE BEAN–PESTO BREAD

This trendy combination is no less appetizing because of its current popularity. Serve this chewy, pungent bread to impress even the most fashionable crowd.

1 lb. Loaf
- ½ cup water
- 2 Tbs. olive oil
- 1 egg
- 3 Tbs. pesto
- ⅓ cup cooked white beans, mashed
- 1 tsp. sugar
- 1 tsp. salt
- ½ cup whole-wheat flour
- 1½ cups bread flour
- 2 Tbs. nonfat dry milk powder
- 1½ tsp. yeast

1½ lb. Loaf
- ¾ cup water
- 3 Tbs. olive oil
- 1½ eggs
- ¼ cup pesto
- ½ cup cooked white beans, mashed
- 2 tsp. sugar
- 1½ tsp. salt
- ⅔ cup whole-wheat flour
- 2⅓ cups bread flour
- 3 Tbs. nonfat dry milk powder
- 2½ tsp. yeast

Bake according to manufacturer's instructions.

CURRIED MANGO CHUTNEY BREAD

This exotic bread is absolutely terrific with cured ham. Also, try adding the almonds for a nice crunchy bite.

1 lb. Loaf
⅔ cup water
1½ Tbs. butter
⅓ cup mango chutney
¾ tsp. curry powder
1 Tbs. sugar
1 tsp. salt
⅔ cup whole-wheat flour
1⅓ cups bread flour
1 tsp. yeast
½ cup unblanched almonds, chopped (optional)

1½ lb. Loaf
1 cup water
2⅓ Tbs. butter
½ cup mango chutney
1 tsp. curry powder
1½ Tbs. sugar
1½ tsp. salt
1 cup whole-wheat flour
2 cups bread flour
1½ tsp. yeast
¾ cup unbalanced almonds, chopped (optional)

Bake according to manufacturer's instructions, adding the optional almonds during the raisin-bread cycle, or five minutes before the final kneading is finished.

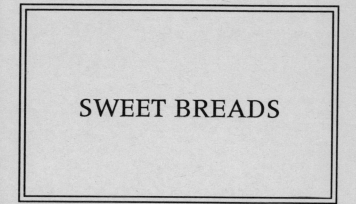

SWEET BREADS

COCONUT ALMOND BREAD

This fragrant sweet bread is a wonderful dessert when served warm with butter melting onto its golden-flecked surface.

1 lb. Loaf
⅔ cup coconut milk
2 Tbs. cream of coconut
⅛ tsp. almond extract
1 Tbs. butter
3 Tbs. almond paste
⅔ tsp. salt
2 cups bread flour
1½ tsp. yeast
½ cup shredded coconut, toasted

1½ lb. Loaf
1 cup coconut milk
3 Tbs. cream of coconut
¼ tsp. almond extract
2 Tbs. butter
¼ cup almond paste
¾ tsp. salt
3 cups bread flour
2½ tsp. yeast
¾ cup shredded coconut, toasted

Bake according to manufacturer's instructions, adding the coconut during the raisin-bread cycle, or five minutes before the final kneading is finished.

CAFE AU LAIT BREAD

Perfect to serve in the afternoon as a pick-me-up, or use de-caffeinated coffee for an evening treat.

1 lb. Loaf
½ cup strong coffee
½ cup milk
4 Tbs. butter
¼ cup sugar
½ tsp. salt
⅓ tsp. cinnamon
2⅔ cups bread flour
1½ tsp. yeast

1½ lb. Loaf
⅔ cup strong coffee
⅔ cup milk
6 Tbs. butter
⅓ cup sugar
¾ tsp. salt
½ tsp. cinnamon
3½ cups bread flour
2½ tsp. yeast

Bake according to manufacturer's instructions.

MEXICAN CHOCOLATE BREAD

Mexican chocolate is typically mixed with cinnamon and made into an unsweetened hot drink served like coffee in the morning. In this bread, I have combined chocolate and cinnamon to approximate that subtle flavor. However, to satisfy modern American palates, I have sweetened it somewhat. If you care to be more traditional, leave out all but one tablespoon of sugar.

1 lb. Loaf
⅔ cup milk
1 egg
4 Tbs. butter
¼ cup sugar
¾ tsp. salt
2 Tbs. unsweetened cocoa
½ tsp. cinnamon
2⅓ cups bread flour
1½ tsp. yeast

1½ lb. Loaf
¾ cup milk
1½ eggs
5 Tbs. butter
⅓ cup sugar
1 tsp. salt
3 Tbs. unsweetened cocoa
¾ tsp. cinnamon
3 cups bread flour
2½ tsp. yeast

Bake according to manufacturer's instructions.

ANISE CREAM BREAD

A golden, rich, smooth loaf that could easily serve as dessert with some sugared strawberries. If you can't find light cream, use half-and-half.

1 lb. Loaf
  ¾ cup light cream
  4 Tbs. butter
  ¼ cup honey
  ½ tsp. salt
  ⅓ tsp. cinnamon
  1 tsp. anise seeds, crushed
  2⅓ cups bread flour
  1½ tsp. yeast

1½ lb. Loaf
  1 cup light cream
  6 Tbs. butter
  ⅓ cup honey
  ¾ tsp. salt
  ½ tsp. cinnamon
  1⅓ tsp. anise seeds, crushed
  3⅛ cups bread flour
  2½ tsp. yeast

Bake according to manufacturer's instructions.

MOCHA HAZELNUT BREAD

This elegant, nutty bread is the best I know to dunk in a frothy cup of cappuccino. If you are very restrained and have any leftovers, soak slices in sweetened coffee and anisette, spread with marscapone cheese (available in Italian specialty shops), and serve as a mock tirame-su. It makes a very decadent and very delicious dessert.

1 lb. Loaf
- ⅔ cup milk
- 2 Tbs. Frangelico liqueur (optional)
- 1 egg
- 4 Tbs. butter
- ¼ cup sugar
- ¾ tsp. salt
- 2 Tbs. unsweetened cocoa
- 2 Tbs. instant espresso powder
- 2½ cups bread flour
- 1½ tsp. yeast
- ⅓ cup chocolate chips
- ⅓ cup toasted hazelnuts, chopped

1½ lb. Loaf
- ¾ cup milk
- 3 Tbs. Frangelico liqueur (optional)
- 1½ eggs
- 5 Tbs. butter
- ⅓ cup sugar
- 1 tsp. salt
- 3 Tbs. unsweetened cocoa
- 3 Tbs. instant espresso powder
- 3¼ cups bread flour
- 2½ tsp. yeast
- ½ cup chocolate chips
- ½ cup toasted hazelnuts, chopped

Bake according to manufacturer's instructions, adding the chocolate chips and hazelnuts during the raisin-bread cycle, or five minutes before the final kneading is finished.

VANILLA BEAN BREAD

The sweet, rich aroma of this bread permeates my whole apartment building, and I love to watch my neighbors lift their noses to breathe in its delicate perfume. Serve this thick, soft bread with jam—it needs no extra butter!

1 lb. Loaf
½ inch long piece of vanilla bean
½ cup heavy cream
2 eggs
4 Tbs. butter
⅓ cup sugar
½ tsp. salt
2½ cups bread flour
1½ tsp. yeast

1½ lb. Loaf
⅔ inch long piece of vanilla bean
⅔ cup heavy cream
2½ eggs
5 Tbs. butter
½ cup sugar
¾ tsp. salt
3⅛ cups bread flour
2½ tsp. yeast

Split the vanilla bean in half lengthwise, and with the point of a small, sharp knife, scrape the seeds out onto a piece of wax paper and reserve. Place the milk in a saucepan over medium-low heat, add the reserved vanilla beans, and gently scald the milk (that is, heat until tiny bubbles appear around the sides of the pan). Do not allow the milk to come to a boil. Remove from heat and cool until the mixture is barely warm to the touch.

Add the cooled milk mixture and the rest of the ingredients to the bread pan, and bake on a sweet bread or regular setting.

OREO COOKIE BREAD

This is great to make for a group of young children, who will adore the smashed cookies marbled throughout each slice. Make sure you serve it with an icy glass of fresh milk.

1 lb. Loaf
- ¾ cup milk
- 1 egg
- 4 Tbs. butter
- 3 Tbs. sugar
- ¾ tsp. salt
- 2 cups bread flour
- 1½ tsp. yeast
- ¾ cup Oreo cookies, crushed

1½ lb. Loaf
- 1 cup milk
- 1½ eggs
- 5 Tbs. butter
- ¼ cup sugar
- 1 tsp. salt
- 3 cups bread flour
- 2½ tsp. yeast
- 1 cup Oreo cookies, crushed

Bake according to manufacturer's instructions, adding the Oreos during the raisin-bread cycle, or five minutes before the final kneading is finished.

SALTED PEANUT–
CHOCOLATE CHIP BREAD

Lovers of chocolate-covered pretzels, come hither! This bread
is a great sweet-salty combination that you can dress up in
myriad ways. Try it with apple slices and melted cheddar
cheese, or with butter and cinnamon sugar—it's terrific.

1 lb. Loaf
- 1 cup milk
- 2 tbs. butter
- 2 Tbs. honey
- ½ cup peanut butter
- ⅔ tsp. salt
- 1 cup whole-wheat flour
- 1½ cups bread flour
- 1½ tsp. yeast
- ½ cup salted peanuts
- ½ cup chocolate chips

1½ lb. Loaf
- 1⅓ cups milk
- 3 Tbs. butter
- 3 Tbs. honey
- ⅔ cup peanut butter
- 1 tsp. salt
- 1⅓ cups whole-wheat flour
- 2 cups bread flour
- 2½ tsp. yeast
- ⅔ cup salted peanuts
- ⅔ cup chocolate chips

Bake according to manufacturer's instructions, adding the peanuts and chocolate chips during the raisin-bread cycle, or five
minutes before the final kneading is finished.

HONEY LEMON BREAD

A moist and delicate loaf that is an unusually delicious way to dress up turkey sandwiches. Use your favorite kind of honey; I use the more robust types like buckwheat or chestnut.

1 lb. Loaf
- ¼ cup water
- 1 cup cottage cheese
- 2 Tbs. butter
- 1 egg
- ¼ cup honey
- 1½ Tbs. freshly grated lemon zest
- ⅔ tsp. salt
- 2½ cups bread flour
- 1½ tsp. yeast

1½ lb. Loaf
- ⅓ cup water
- 1¼ cups cottage cheese
- 2½ Tbs. butter
- 1½ eggs
- ⅓ cup honey
- 2 Tbs. freshly grated lemon zest
- 1 tsp. salt
- 3 cups bread flour
- 2½ tsp. yeast

Bake according to manufacturer's instructions.

SWEET SAFFRON BREAD

This delicately perfumed loaf was developed to accompany a steaming cup of cinnamon tea with milk and sugar. Rosewater is available at specialty shops, drugstores (sold as a facial tonic), and sometimes in liquor stores. Use whole cardamom pods and remove the black seeds inside the casing.

1 lb. Loaf
- ¾ cup milk
- ¼ tsp. saffron threads
- ¼ cup rosewater
- 2 Tbs. butter
- 3 Tbs. honey
- 1 tsp. salt
- ½ tsp. cinnamon
- ½ tsp. cardamom seeds, crushed
- ⅛ tsp. ground cloves
- 3 cups bread flour
- 1½ tsp. yeast
- ⅔ cup golden raisins

1½ lb. Loaf
- 1 cup milk
- ⅓ tsp. saffron threads
- ⅓ cup rosewater
- 3 Tbs. butter
- ¼ cup honey
- 1½ tsp. salt
- ⅔ tsp. cinnamon
- ⅔ tsp. cardamom seeds, crushed
- scant ¼ tsp. ground cloves
- 4 cups bread flour
- 2½ tsp. yeast
- ¾ cup golden raisins

Heat the milk and saffron in a saucepan until the milk is scalded (that is, until bubbles appear around the edges of the pan). Remove from heat and allow to cool until it feels barely warm to the touch.

Add to the bread pan with the other ingredients, and bake according to manufacturer's instructions, adding the raisins during the raisin-bread cycle, or five minutes before the final kneading is finished.

JULBROD

This bread is traditionally served in Sweden at Christmas time. It is a rich, spicy loaf that I love to eat for breakfast, toasted with orange marmalade. Use whole cardamom pods, and remove the tiny black seeds within. If you cannot find them, you may substitute cardamom powder, but the flavor is nowhere near as delectable.

1 lb. Loaf
- ¾ cup milk
- 1 egg
- ½ tsp. vanilla extract
- ¼ tsp. almond extract
- 6 Tbs. butter
- ¼ cup honey
- ¾ tsp. salt
- 1 tsp. cardamom seeds, crushed
- ¼ tsp. ground cloves
- 2¼ cups bread flour
- 1½ tsp. yeast
- ⅓ cup currants
- ¼ cup golden raisins
- ¼ cup slivered almonds

1½ lb. Loaf
- 1 cup milk
- 1½ eggs
- ¾ tsp. vanilla extract
- ⅓ tsp. almond extract
- 8 Tbs. butter
- ⅓ cup honey
- 1 tsp. salt
- 1½ tsp. cardamom seeds, crushed
- ⅓ tsp. ground cloves
- 3 cups bread flour
- 2½ tsp. yeast
- ½ cup currants
- ⅓ cup golden raisins
- ⅓ cup slivered almonds

Bake according to manufacturer's instructions, adding the currants, almonds, and raisins during the raisin-bread cycle, or five minutes before the final kneading is finished.

MARMALADE BREAD

Another succulent breakfast bread that is nicely enhanced with a little butter. Use any flavor marmalade you like; aside from orange, I've made this bread with grapefruit, three-fruit, and lemon marmalade—all with super results.

1 lb. Loaf
⅔ cup water
1½ Tbs. butter
⅓ cup marmalade
1 Tbs. honey
⅔ tsp. salt
⅔ cup whole-wheat flour
1⅓ cups bread flour
1 tsp. yeast

1½ lb. Loaf
1 cup water
2⅓ Tbs. butter
½ cup marmalade
1½ Tbs. honey
¾ tsp. salt
1 cup whole-wheat flour
2 cups bread flour
1½ tsp. yeast

Bake according to manufacturer's instructions.

PRESERVED GINGER BREAD

This is a terrific loaf to wake up to. Set your timer, and the spicy smell will entice even the most ardent oversleepers out of dreamland. Ginger preserves and preserved ginger in syrup are slightly different, but can be used interchangeably in this recipe. The optional crystallized ginger adds nice intense pockets of ginger, but is for serious ginger lovers only.

1 lb. Loaf
 ⅔ cup water
1½ Tbs. butter
 ⅓ cup ginger preserves or preserved ginger in syrup
 1 Tbs. sugar
 ⅔ tsp. salt
 ⅔ cup whole-wheat flour
1⅓ cups bread flour
 1 tsp. yeast
 ½ cup chopped crystallized ginger (optional)

1½ lb. Loaf
 1 cup water
2⅓ Tbs. butter
 ½ cup ginger preserves or preserved ginger in syrup
1½ Tbs. sugar
 ¾ tsp. salt
 1 cup whole-wheat flour
 2 cups bread flour
1½ tsp. yeast
 ¾ cup chopped crystallized ginger (optional)

Bake according to manufacturer's instructions, adding the optional crystallized ginger during the raisin-bread cycle, or five minutes before the final kneading is finished.

PORT WINE SOAKED FIG BREAD

A deeply flavored, rich loaf that is elegant enough for your most important company. It makes an absolutely stunning gift, especially around the holiday season.

1 lb. Loaf
½ cup port
¾ cup dried figs, cut into quarters
¾ cup plain yogurt
2 Tbs. butter
3 Tbs. honey
¾ tsp. salt
½ cup whole-wheat flour
½ cup cornmeal
2 cups bread flour
2 Tbs. nonfat dry milk powder
1½ tsp. yeast

1½ lb. Loaf
⅔ cup port
1 cup dried figs, cut into quarters
1 cup plain yogurt
3 Tbs. butter
¼ cup honey
1 tsp. salt
⅔ cup whole-wheat flour
⅔ cup cornmeal
2⅔ cups bread flour
3 Tbs. nonfat dry milk powder
2½ tsp. yeast

Soak the figs in the port for at least one hour. When the figs have absorbed a good deal of the liquid, add whatever port is left to the bread pan. Reserve the figs for later.

Add the rest of the ingredients to the pan, and bake according to manufacturer's instructions. Add the figs during the raisin-bread cycle, or five minutes before the final kneading is finished.

ITALIAN MARSALA BREAD

The recipe for this sweet bread was adapted from my favorite cookie recipe. I adore the combination of the chewy, Marsala-fattened raisins against the sandy texture of cornmeal. To quote one of my more eloquent tasters, this loaf is "eminently man-ductable." It also is a much-appreciated gift.

1 lb. Loaf
½ cup dry Marsala
¾ cup golden raisins
¾ cup milk
4 Tbs. butter
3 Tbs. honey
¾ tsp. salt
1 cup cornmeal
2 cups bread flour
1½ tsp. yeast

1½ lb. Loaf
⅔ cup dry Marsala
1 cup golden raisins
1 cup milk
5 Tbs. butter
¼ cup honey
1 tsp. salt
1⅓ cups cornmeal
2⅔ cups bread flour
2½ tsp. yeast

Soak the raisins in the Marsala for at least thirty minutes. When the raisins have absorbed a good deal of the liquid, add whatever Marsala is left to the bread pan. Reserve the raisins for later.

Place the rest of the ingredients into the pan, and bake according to manufacturer's instructions. Add the raisins during the raisin-bread cycle, or five minutes before the final kneading is finished.

CALYPSO BREAD

Bright and tart-sweet, this is great, as you can imagine, with Caribbean food. Coconut milk can be found in specialty-food shops and large supermarkets—do not confuse it with cream of coconut, which is much thicker and sweeter. If you can find desiccated coconut in your nearby health-food store, use it instead of the standard supermarket flaked coconut, which contains abundant sugar.

1 lb. Loaf
- 1 cup coconut milk
- 2 Tbs. vegetable oil
- 2 Tbs. brown sugar
- 1 Tbs. grated lime rind
- 1 tsp. salt
- 3 cups bread flour
- ¼ cup nonfat dry milk powder
- 1½ tsp. yeast
- ⅔ cup flaked coconut, toasted

1½ lb. Loaf
- 1⅓ cups coconut milk
- 3 Tbs. vegetable oil
- 3 Tbs. brown sugar
- 1⅓ Tbs. grated lime rind
- 1½ tsp. salt
- 4 cups bread flour
- ⅓ cup nonfat dry milk powder
- 2½ tsp. yeast
- ¾ cup flaked coconut, toasted

Bake according to manufacturer's instructions, adding the coconut during the raisin-bread cycle, or five minutes before the final kneading is finished.

GOLDEN BREAD

This magnificent bread is fine enough to serve royalty. The secret ingredient is refiner's syrup, sold as Lyle's Golden Syrup, which can be purchased from specialty-food shops.

1 lb. Loaf
⅔ cup milk
1 egg
4 Tbs. butter
¼ cup refiner's syrup
½ tsp. salt
2⅔ cups bread flour
1½ tsp. yeast
½ cup golden raisins

1½ lb. Loaf
¾ cup milk
1½ eggs
6 Tbs. butter
⅓ cup refiner's syrup
¾ tsp. salt
3½ cups bread flour
2½ tsp. yeast
⅔ cup golden raisins

Bake according to manufacturer's instructions, adding the raisins during the raisin-bread cycle, or five minutes before the final kneading is finished.

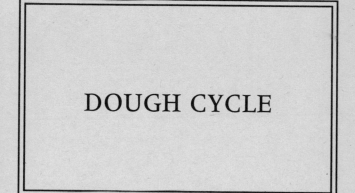

DOUGH CYCLE

FRENCH BAGUETTES

Crispy baguettes are next to impossible to find well made outside of France, unless of course you make them yourself. Here is a relatively simple way to bake spectacular loaves—your guests will swear you flew them in specially from Paris.

1 lb. Loaf
- ¾ cup water
- 1 tsp. sugar
- 1 tsp. salt
- 2 cups bread flour
- 1½ tsp. yeast

1½ lb. Loaf
- 1 cup water
- 1½ tsp. sugar
- 1½ tsp. salt
- 3 cups bread flour
- 2 tsp. yeast

Set bread machine on the dough cycle. When the dough is ready, remove it from the bread machine and divide into two or three pieces, depending upon how long you would like your baguettes to be. Roll with your hands into skinny wands, and place on a baking sheet, or pizza stone if you have one, that has been sprinkled generously with cornmeal. With a very sharp knife, slash the tops of the baguettes with three diagonal cuts.

Cover the bread with a dish towel or plastic wrap, and let rise in a warm place for thirty to forty-five minutes, until doubled in bulk.

Place the bread in an oven preheated to 450 degrees. Bake for twelve to fifteen minutes, depending upon how thick the loaves are. When properly done, the loaves should have a deep brown crust (not burned) and sound hollow when tapped.

To achieve a crispier crust, you will want to create steam in the oven while the baguettes bake. There are several ways to do this. The easiest is to put a pan of water on the bottom of the oven while the loaves bake. The best way is to periodically spray the loaves with water from a plant mister. Personally, I like to throw ice cubes into the oven at the beginning and middle of the baking.

Another way to produce a crisp crust is to brush the tops of the baguettes with beaten egg white. This will also make it shiny. If you do this, you don't need to mist the loaves, but the results will be different.

Try all these methods and see which produces the best crust for your taste. Just remember not to open the oven more than a crack for misting and throwing ice cubes in, otherwise too much heat will escape.

CRUSTY SOURDOUGH BAGUETTES

Sourdough baguettes should be formed as thin as possible so that they're almost all crust—the very best part! Because of the milk in the starter, this bread stays fresh longer than your average French baguette.

1 lb. Loaf
- ⅔ **cup sour starter (see page 14)**
- ⅓ **cup water**
- 1 **tsp. sugar**
- 1 **tsp. salt**
- 2 **cups bread flour**
- 1 **tsp. yeast**

1½ lb. Loaf
- 1 **cup sour starter (see page 14)**
- ⅔ **cup water**
- 2 **tsp. sugar**
- 1½ **tsp. salt**
- 3 **cups bread flour**
- 1½ **tsp. yeast**

Set bread machine on the dough cycle. When the dough is ready, remove it from the bread machine and divide into two or three pieces, depending upon how long you would like your baguettes to be. Roll with your hands into the skinniest wands possible, and place on a baking sheet, or pizza stone if you have one, that has been sprinkled generously with cornmeal. With a very sharp knife, slash the tops of the baguettes with three diagonal cuts.

Cover bread with a dish towel or plastic wrap, and let rise in a warm place for thirty to forty-five minutes, until doubled in bulk.

Place the bread in an oven preheated to 450 degrees. Bake for twelve to fifteen minutes, depending upon how thick the loaves are. When properly done, the loaves should have a deep brown crust (not burned) and sound hollow when tapped.

To achieve a crispier crust, you will want to create steam in the oven while the baguettes bake. There are several ways to do this. The easiest is to put a pan of water on the bottom of the oven while the loaves bake. The best way is to periodically spray the loaves with water from a plant mister. Personally, I like to throw ice cubes into the oven at the beginning and middle of the baking.

Another way to produce a crisp crust is to brush the tops of the baguettes with beaten egg white. This will also make it shiny. If you do this, you don't need to mist the loaves, but the results will be different.

Try all these methods and see which produces the best crust for your taste. Just remember not to open the oven more than a crack for misting and throwing ice cubes in, otherwise too much heat will escape.

ONION SOURDOUGH BAGUETTES

These savory loaves are just terrific for everything. And very elegant, too.

1 lb. Loaf
⅔ cup sour starter (see page 14)
⅓ cup water
1 tsp. sugar
1 tsp. salt
2 cups bread flour
1 tsp. yeast
¼ cup sautéed onion

1½ lb. Loaf
1 cup sour starter (see page 14)
⅔ cup water
2 tsp. sugar
1½ tsp. salt

3 cups bread flour
1½ tsp. yeast
⅓ cup sautéed onion

Put all ingredients into bread pan except onions. Set bread machine on the dough cycle. When the dough is ready, remove it from the bread machine and divide into two or three pieces, depending upon how long you would like your baguettes to be. Roll with your hands into the skinniest wands possible, and place on a baking sheet, or pizza stone if you have one, that has been sprinkled generously with cornmeal. With a very sharp knife, slash the tops of the baguettes with three diagonal cuts.

Cover bread with a dish towel or plastic wrap, and let rise in a warm place for thirty to forty-five minutes, until doubled in bulk.

Brush bread crusts with water and sprinkle on the onions. Place the bread in an oven preheated to 450 degrees. Bake for twelve to fifteen minutes, depending upon how thick the loaves are. When properly done, the loaves should have a deep brown crust (not burned) and sound hollow when tapped.

To achieve a crispier crust, you will want to create steam in the oven while the baguettes bake. There are several ways to do this. The easiest is to put a pan of water on the bottom of the oven while the loaves bake. The best way is to periodically spray the loaves with water from a plant mister. Personally, I like to throw ice cubes into the oven at the beginning and middle of the baking.

Try all these methods and see which produces the best crust for your taste. Just remember not to open the oven more than a crack for misting and throwing ice cubes in, otherwise too much heat will escape.

WHOLE-WHEAT BAGUETTES

Try this full-flavored, crunchy baguette with your favorite cheese and fresh, ripe fruit to end an important meal. The optional caraway seeds, usually reserved for rye breads, combine pleasantly with whole wheat.

1 lb. Loaf
 ¾ cup water
 2 tsp. brown sugar
 1 tsp. salt
 1 cup whole-wheat flour
 1 cup bread flour
 1 tsp. gluten
1½ tsp. yeast
 ¾ tsp. caraway seeds (optional)

1½ lb. Loaf
 1 cup water
 1 Tbs. brown sugar
1½ tsp. salt
1½ cup whole-wheat flour
1½ cups bread flour
1½ tsp. gluten
 2 tsp. yeast
 1 tsp. caraway seeds (optional)

Set bread machine on the dough cycle. When the dough is ready, remove it from the bread machine and divide into two or three pieces, depending upon how long you would like your baguettes to be. Roll with your hands into skinny wands, and place on a baking sheet, or pizza stone if you have one, that has been sprinkled generously with cornmeal. With a very sharp knife, slash the tops of the baguettes with three diagonal cuts.

Cover the bread with a dish towel or plastic wrap, and let rise in a warm place for thirty to forty-five minutes, until doubled in bulk.

Place the bread in an oven preheated to 450 degrees. Bake for twelve to fifteen minutes, depending upon how thick the loaves are. When properly done, the loaves should have a deep brown crust (not burned) and sound hollow when tapped.

To achieve a crispier crust, you will want to create steam in the oven while the baguettes bake. There are several ways to do this. The easiest is to put a pan of water on the bottom of the oven while the loaves bake. The best way is to periodically spray the loaves with water from a plant mister. Personally, I like to throw ice cubes into the oven at the beginning and middle of the baking.

Another way to produce a crisp crust is to brush the tops of the baguettes with beaten egg white. This will also make it shiny. If you do this, you don't need to mist the loaves, but the results will be different.

Try all these methods and see which produces the best crust for your taste. Just remember not to open the oven more than a crack for misting and throwing ice cubes in, otherwise too much heat will escape.

BUTTERMILK OATMEAL ROLLS

Soft, luscious rolls that are perfect for sandwiches.

10 Rolls
1¼ cups buttermilk
2 Tbs. butter
1 Tbs. sugar
1½ tsp. salt
1 cup oatmeal plus extra for sprinkling on the tops
2 cups bread flour
1½ tsp. yeast
milk for brushing the tops

15 Rolls
1⅔ cups buttermilk
3 Tbs. butter
1½ Tbs. sugar
2 tsp. salt
1½ cups oatmeal plus extra for sprinkling on the tops
2½ cups bread flour
2½ tsp. yeast
milk for brushing the tops

Set bread machine on the dough cycle. When the dough is ready, remove it from the bread machine, divide into the corresponding number of balls and place on a baking sheet.

Cover with a dish towel or plastic wrap, and set in a warm place to rise for forty-five to sixty minutes, until double in bulk.

Brush the tops with milk and sprinkle with oatmeal. Place the rolls in an oven preheated to 375 degrees. Bake for eighteen to twenty minutes. When properly done, the rolls should be golden brown.

KAISER ROLLS

Although these rolls do not have the twisted pattern on top, they taste every bit as good as the best crispy kaiser roll.

6 Rolls
 ¾ cup milk
 1 egg
 1 Tbs. butter
 1 Tbs. sugar
 1 tsp. salt
2⅓ cups bread flour
1½ tsp. yeast
   poppy seeds for sprinkling on top

15 Rolls
1½ cups milk
1½ eggs
1½ Tbs. butter
1½ Tbs. sugar
1½ tsp. salt
4½ cups bread flour
2½ tsp. yeast
   poppy seeds for sprinkling on top

Set bread machine on the dough cycle. When the dough is ready, remove it from the bread machine, divide into the corresponding number of balls, and flatten with your hands until the dough is about a half inch thick. Place on a baking sheet.

Cover with a dish towel or plastic wrap, and set in a warm place to rise for forty-five minutes, until double in bulk.

Brush the tops with water and sprinkle with poppy seeds. Place the rolls in an oven preheated to 425 degrees. Bake for twenty to twenty-five minutes. When properly done, the rolls should be golden brown, and sound hollow when tapped.

WHOLE-GRAIN ROLLS

These nutty rolls are excellent for picnics and to make sandwiches with. They are crusty on the outside and soft within.

10–12 Rolls

1¼ cups water
2 Tbs. vegetable oil
1 Tbs. molasses
1½ tsp. salt
2 Tbs. flax seeds
¼ cup wheat germ
¼ cup oatmeal
¼ cup rye flour
⅔ cup whole-wheat flour
1½ cups bread flour
2 Tbs. nonfat dry milk powder
1 tsp. gluten
1½ tsp. yeast

14–16 Rolls

1⅔ cups water
3 Tbs. vegetable oil
1½ Tbs. molasses
2 tsp. salt
3 Tbs. flax seeds
⅓ cup wheat germ
⅓ cup oatmeal
⅓ cup rye flour
¾ cup whole-wheat flour
2 cups bread flour
3 Tbs. nonfat dry milk powder
1½ tsp. gluten
2½ tsp. yeast

Set bread machine on the dough cycle. When the dough is ready, remove it from the bread machine and divide into the corresponding number of balls and place on a baking sheet.

Cover with a dish towel or plastic wrap, and set in a warm place to rise for forty-five to sixty minutes, until double in bulk.

Place the rolls in an oven preheated to 400 degrees. Bake for fifteen to twenty minutes. When properly done, the rolls should sound hollow when tapped.

WHOLE-WHEAT RAISIN NUT ROLLS

I like to make these rolls very small so the outside is covered in raisins and nuts, which toast nicely in the oven's heat. They are perfect dinner-party fare.

14 Rolls
¾ cup water
½ cup milk
2 Tbs. butter
1 Tbs. honey
1½ tsp. salt
1½ cups whole-wheat flour
1½ cups bread flour
2 Tbs. nonfat dry milk powder
1½ tsp. yeast
½ cup raisins
½ cup walnuts

18 Rolls
1 cup water
⅔ cup milk
3 Tbs. butter
1½ Tbs. honey
2 tsp. salt
2 cups whole-wheat flour
2 cups bread flour
3 Tbs. nonfat dry milk powder
2½ tsp. yeast
⅔ cup raisins
⅔ cup walnuts

Add all ingredients except raisins and nuts to bread pan, and set on the dough cycle. When the dough is ready, remove it from the bread machine and knead in the raisins and nuts. Divide dough into the corresponding number of balls and place on a baking sheet.

Cover with a dish towel or plastic wrap, and set in a warm place to rise for thirty to forty-five minutes, until double in bulk.

Place the rolls in an oven preheated to 400 degrees. Bake for ten to fifteen minutes. When properly done, the rolls should sound hollow when tapped.

PITA POCKETS

If you have never made your own pita breads, you are in for a treat. These breads are chewy little disks that puff up while baking, creating the pocket. Stuff them with any sandwich filling of your choice, and bring them with you for lunch. I like to make them part whole-wheat flour, but if you would rather have them all white, go ahead and replace the whole-wheat flour with bread flour.

6 Pitas
   1 cup water
   2 Tbs. vegetable oil
   1 tsp. sugar
   1 tsp. salt
   1 cup whole-wheat flour
   1 cup bread flour
1½ tsp. yeast

8 Pitas
1¼ cups water
2½ Tbs. vegetable oil
1½ tsp. sugar
1½ tsp. salt
1½ cups whole-wheat flour
1½ cups bread flour
2½ tsp. yeast

Set bread machine on the dough cycle. When the dough is ready, remove it from the bread machine, divide into the corresponding number of balls. Roll each ball as thin as possible with a rolling pin. Place on a baking sheet.

Cover with a dish towel or plastic wrap, and set in a warm place to rise for twenty minutes.

Place the pitas in an oven preheated to 500 degrees. Bake for five to eight minutes, until the tops brown and the pitas puff up.

CORN STICKS

These golden-brown, mealy treats are fun to serve outdoors at a barbecue, or to have around the house for snacks.

14 Sticks
- 1 cup milk
- ¼ cup vegetable oil
- 3 Tbs. honey
- 1½ tsp. salt
- 1 cup cornmeal
- 2 cups bread flour
- 1½ tsp. yeast
- melted butter for brushing the tops

18 Sticks
- 1⅓ cups milk
- ⅓ cup vegetable oil
- ¼ cup honey
- 2 tsp. salt
- 1½ cups cornmeal
- 2½ cups bread flour
- 2½ tsp. yeast
- melted butter for brushing the tops

Set bread machine on the dough cycle. When the dough is ready, remove it from the bread machine, roll into the corresponding number of sticks and place on a baking sheet.

Cover with a dish towel or plastic wrap, and set in a warm place to rise for thirty to forty-five minutes, until double in bulk.

Brush the tops with the melted butter, and place the corn sticks in an oven preheated to 375 degrees. Bake for twelve to fifteen minutes, or until pale gold on top.

MAPLE WALNUT STICKY BUNS

These should be called gooey buns because the rich, nutty filling oozing out of the center makes them more than just sticky. Serve them right of the oven for a splendid treat. If you cannot procure maple sugar, use light brown sugar instead.

12 Buns
 ¾ **cup milk**
 2 **eggs**
 4 **Tbs. butter**
 ⅓ **cup maple sugar**
1½ **tsp. lemon zest**
 1 **tsp. cinnamon**
 ½ **tsp. freshly grated nutmeg**
 1 **tsp. salt**
3½ **cups bread flour**
2½ **tsp. yeast**

Add all ingredients to the bread pan and set on the dough cycle.

Filling
 ¼ **cup maple sugar**
 1 **tsp. cinnamon**
 ¾ **cup walnuts, chopped**
 ⅓ **cup raisins**

Mix all ingredients together in a bowl and reserve.

Glaze
 ¾ **cup maple sugar**
 ⅓ **cup maple syrup**
 ¾ **cup melted butter**
 ⅓ **cup milk**
 1 **cup walnuts**

Mix all ingredients together in a bowl and reserve.
 Prepare a nine by thirteen-inch baking pan by buttering the bottom and sides well. Evenly spread the topping on the bottom. Set aside.

When the dough is ready, remove it from the bread machine and roll out into a rectangle about one-third-inch thick. Sprinkle on the filling mixture and press into the dough with your hands. Starting on one side, roll up the dough tightly. Cut the dough into three-quarter-inch slices and place in the prepared pan cut side down. Leave enough room between the slices so that they have room to rise.

Cover with a dish towel or plastic wrap, and set in a warm place to rise for thirty to forty-five minutes, until double in bulk.

Place the buns in an oven preheated to 350 degrees. Bake for thirty minutes or until brown. Carefully invert the pan onto a platter, and serve immediately.

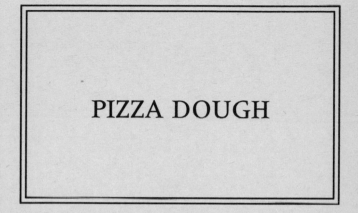

PIZZA DOUGH

PIZZA TIPS

Making a good pizza is quite easy with the bread machine, and demands very little planning on your part. Just mix up the dough in the machine, roll it out, top with anything you have, and bake.

You can also make the dough in advance, refrigerate it, and come back to it later when you are ready to bake. Dough will keep, tightly covered, in the refrigerator for two days. Just bring it to room temperature (this can be done in a microwave very efficiently), and proceed where you left off. Pizza dough, and completely baked pizzas, will also freeze well, and are nice to have on hand.

If you happen to have a pizza stone and pizza peel (which is a large, flat wooden spatula that they use in real pizzerias to carry the unbaked pizza into the oven), or love pizza enough to buy them, they will make your pizza taste like it came out of a brick oven. The crust will be extra golden and crispy, and the toppings just slightly brown.

The pizza stone is an unglazed, circular ceramic tile that should be preheated with the oven for at least forty-five minutes. Prepare the pizza directly on the peel (which should be heavily coated with cornmeal so the pizza won't stick to it), and then slide the pie onto the hot stone. The stone retains and distributes heat more efficiently than a regular oven. Also, you needn't grease the stone, just coat with cornmeal. And be very careful when taking the pizza out of the oven, the stone is *hot!*

QUICK AND EASY PIZZA DOUGH

What a joy to be able to make homemade pizza without fuss. This basic dough can be used with most any pizza topping I list, or with any you can think up. This pizza recipe makes one fourteen-inch pizza serving four.

⅔ cup water
1½ Tbs. olive oil
½ tsp. salt
2 cups bread flour
1½ tsp. yeast

Put all ingredients in the bread pan and set the machine on the dough cycle. When the dough is finished, remove from the pan, cover with a dish towel or plastic wrap, and allow to rest for fifteen minutes.

Roll or stretch the dough into a fourteen-inch circle. Place on an oiled baking sheet, or on a pizza peel well coated with cornmeal.

Top with the topping combination of your choice, and bake in a preheated, 500-degree oven for fifteen to twenty minutes until the crust is golden and the toppings bubbling.

WHOLE-WHEAT PIZZA DOUGH

Whole-wheat flour makes a chewier, more robust pizza crust that is a nice change from the usual. You can use this crust with any topping, but it works best with full-flavored ones like the meat sauce and the pesto. This pizza recipe makes one fourteen-inch pizza serving four.

⅔ cup water
1½ Tbs. olive oil
½ tsp. salt
1 cup whole-wheat flour
1 cup bread flour
1½ tsp. yeast

Put all ingredients in the bread pan and set the machine on the dough cycle. When the dough is finished, remove from the pan, cover with a dish towel or plastic wrap, and allow to rest for fifteen minutes.

Roll or stretch the dough into a fourteen-inch circle. Place on an oiled baking sheet, or on a pizza peel well coated with cornmeal.

Top with the topping combination of your choice, and bake in a preheated, 500-degree oven for fifteen to twenty minutes until the crust is golden and the toppings bubbling.

CLASSIC PIZZA SAUCE

This wonderful pizza will satisfy everyone looking for a light but luscious slice.

Sauce

    1 **28 oz. can peeled plum tomatoes**
    2 **cloves garlic, minced**
¼–½ **tsp. hot pepper flakes, to taste (optional)**
    2 **tsp. olive oil**
    1 **Tbs. fresh Italian parsley, minced**
    1 **Tbs. fresh basil, chopped**
    Salt and freshly ground black pepper, to taste

Combine the tomatoes, garlic, optional hot pepper, and olive oil in a saucepan, and simmer on low heat, stirring to break up the tomatoes, for thirty minutes.

Add seasoning and herbs, and simmer for another five minutes.

Spread the sauce on the prepared pizza crust of your choice, and top with any or all of the following:

    Sliced fresh or sauteed mushrooms
    Chopped green or red peppers
    Sliced onion
    Black olives
    Sautéed Italian sausage, crumbled
    Shredded prosciutto
    Cooked bacon
    Baked eggplant slices
    Etc., etc.
1½–2½ **cups grated mozzarella, to taste**
    ¼ **cup imported Parmesan cheese**

If you are using cheese, sprinkle it over the other toppings, and bake as directed.

HEARTY SAUSAGE PIZZA SAUCE

Great for light winter dinners teamed with a large salad. This
one is perfect to bake on a whole-wheat crust.

Sauce
- ½ lb. hot Italian sausage, sautéed and crumbled
- 1 28 oz. can peeled plum tomatoes
- 2 cloves garlic, minced
- ½–1 tsp. hot pepper flakes
- 2 tsp. olive oil
- 2 Tbs. fresh Italian parsley, minced
- Salt and freshly ground black pepper, to taste

Combine the sausage, tomatoes, garlic, hot pepper flakes, and
olive oil in a saucepan, and simmer on low heat, stirring to
break up the tomatoes, for thirty minutes.

Add seasoning and parsley, and simmer for another five
minutes.

Spread the sauce on the prepared pizza crust of your choice,
and top with:

- 1 red or green bell pepper, thinly sliced
- ½ cup thinly sliced onion
- 2 Tbs. capers
- 1½–2½ cups grated mozzarella, to taste
- ¼ cup imported Parmesan cheese

Evenly spread pepper, onion, and capers over the sauce. Sprinkle with cheese and bake as directed.

PISSILARDIERE

This lusty pie is a Provençal variation on pizza. If you must leave out the anchovies, double the amount of olives.

- 2 cups onions, sliced very thin
- 2 Tbs. olive oil
- ¼ cup Niçoise olives
- ¼ cup fresh thyme leaves
- 6–10 whole anchovy fillets, to taste
  Salt and freshly ground black pepper, to taste

Sauté the onions very gently in the oil until they are golden. Spread them on the quick and easy pizza crust (page 176) and top with olives and thyme. Decorate with the anchovies and season to taste. Bake as directed.

PESTO PIZZA

Bright green and terrifically herby, I love this as an appetizer to a summer meal.

- 1 cup pesto
- ½ cup ricotta cheese
- 1 cup mozzarella cheese, grated
- 10 whole basil leaves

Spread any pizza crust of your choice with pesto. Top with ricotta cheese and sprinkle with mozzarella. Bake as directed. Decorate with whole basil leaves.

SEAFOOD PIZZA

Because most seafood cooks quickly, it will not need to be precooked before adding to the crust. This combination is only a suggestion, substitute as you please.

 1 cup tomato sauce for classic pizza (see page 178)
10 large shrimp, cleaned
 4 oz. bay scallops
½ cup fresh lump crabmeat
¼ cup black olives
½ cup shredded basil leaves
   Salt and freshly ground black pepper, to taste

Spread the sauce on any pizza crust, top with seafood and olives. Season to taste and bake as directed. Top with basil leaves.

BLUE CHEESE–PEAR PIZZA

A very sophisticated way to eat pizza. The walnuts add a nice crunch.

 1 large pear, sliced thinly
 1 cup blue cheese, crumbled
½ cup walnut halves
   Freshly ground black pepper, to taste

Decoratively arrange the pear slices on top of a pizza crust. Top with blue cheese, walnuts, and pepper. Bake as directed.

FRESH HERB AND ONION PIZZA

This light pizza is the very essence of summer. Vidalia onions are a very mild and sweet variety grown in Georgia. They are available in specialty-food stores nationwide.

  1 **cup sweet vidalia onion, sliced very thinly**
  ½ **cup fresh Italian parsley, minced**
  ½ **cup fresh thyme leaves**
  ½ **cup shredded basil leaves**
  ¼ **cup fresh rosemary**
    Olive oil for drizzling
    Salt and freshly ground black pepper, to taste

Spread the onions and then the herbs on any pizza crust, drizzle with olive oil, and season to taste. Bake as directed.

PRIMAVERA PIZZA

A creamy blend of cheese and vegetables that is guaranteed to please everybody.

  1 **cup tomato sauce for classic pizza (page 178)**
  ½ **cup ricotta cheese**
  ½ **cup cooked broccoli florets**
  ½ **cup cooked white beans**
  1 **red or yellow bell pepper, thinly sliced**
  ½ **cup thinly sliced onion**
⅓–½ **cup freshly grated Parmesan cheese, to taste**
    Salt and freshly ground black pepper, to taste
  ½ **cup fresh basil, shredded**

Spread the tomato sauce on any pizza crust, and top with ricotta cheese and vegetables. Sprinkle Parmesan over the vegetables, season to taste, and bake as directed. Top with basil leaves.

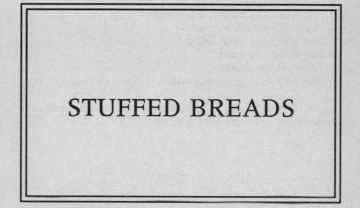

STUFFED BREADS

SAUSAGE STUFFED HERB BREAD

I serve this one directly out of the machine for an easy supper.

1 lb. Loaf
- ¾ cup milk
- 2 Tbs. olive oil
- 1 tsp. sugar
- 1 egg
- ½ cup combination any chopped fresh herbs of your choice
- 1 tsp. salt
- 2 cups bread flour
- 1½ tsp. yeast

Filling
- ½ cup cooked Italian sausage, crumbled

1½ lb. Loaf
- 1 cup milk
- 3 Tbs. olive oil
- 1½ eggs
- 2 tsp. sugar
- 1½ tsp. salt
- ⅔ cup combination any chopped fresh herbs of your choice
- 3 cups bread flour
- 2½ tsp. yeast

Filling
- ⅔ cup cooked Italian sausage, crumbled

1. Set aside sausage for filling.
2. Bake the loaf according to manufacturer's instructions. About ten or fifteen minutes before the rising period is over, stick your fingers into the dough and make a hole big enough to accommodate the filling. *Do not* use a knife for this, or you will rupture the gluten. Carefully spoon the filling in the hole. Leave to finish rising and baking. Cool on a rack.

STUFFED SALSA CORN BREAD

Wonderful all by its lonesome for lunch.

1 lb. Loaf
- ¾ cup milk
- ¼ cup olive oil
- 1 egg
- 1 tsp. sugar
- ½ tsp. salt
- 1 cup cornmeal
- 1 cup bread flour
- 1½ tsp. yeast

Filling
- ½ cup chunky salsa, extra liquid drained off
- ½ cup grated mozzarella cheese

1½ lb. Loaf
- 1 cup milk
- ⅓ cup olive oil
- 1½ eggs
- 2 tsp. sugar
- ¾ tsp. salt
- 1½ cups cornmeal
- 1½ cups bread flour
- 2½ tsp. yeast

Filling
- ⅔ cup chunky salsa, extra liquid drained off
- ⅔ cup grated mozzarella cheese

1. Mix the filling ingredients together and set aside.
2. Bake the loaf according to manufacturer's instructions. About ten or fifteen minutes before the rising period is over, stick your fingers into the dough and make a hole big enough to accommodate the filling. *Do not* use a knife for this, or you will rupture the gluten. Carefully spoon the filling in the hole. Leave to finish rising and baking. Cool on a rack.

STUFFED WHOLE-WHEAT
APPLE BREAD

A tasty, healthy snack. Serve hot slices with cold milk.

1 lb. Loaf
- ⅔ cup milk
- 1 egg
- 2 Tbs. butter
- 3 Tbs. molasses
- 1 tsp. cardamom
- ½ tsp. salt
- 1 cup whole-wheat flour
- 1 cup bread flour
- 1½ tsp. yeast

Filling
- ½ cup apples, diced
- 2 Tbs. honey
- 1 tsp. cinnamon
- ¼ cup golden raisins

1½ lb. Loaf
- ¾ cup milk
- 1½ eggs
- 2½ Tbs. butter
- ¼ cup molasses
- 1½ tsp. cardamom
- ¾ tsp. salt
- 1½ cups whole-wheat flour
- 1½ cups bread flour
- 2½ tsp. yeast

Filling
- ⅔ cup apples, diced
- 3 Tbs. honey
- 1 tsp. cinnamon
- ⅓ cup golden raisins

1. Mix all the filling ingredients together and set aside.
2. Bake the loaf according to manufacturer's instructions.

About ten or fifteen minutes before the rising period is over, stick your fingers into the dough and make a hole big enough to accommodate the filling. *Do not* use a knife for this, or you will rupture the gluten. Carefully spoon the filling in the hole. Leave to finish rising and baking. Cool on a rack.

STUFFED PEACH BREAD

This delightful bread tastes like a peach turnover. Use only fresh, ripe peaches for the best flavor and texture.

1 lb. Loaf
¾ cup milk
1 egg
2 Tbs. butter
3 Tbs. sugar
2 tsp. cinnamon
½ tsp. salt
2 cups bread flour
1½ tsp. yeast

Filling
½ cup peaches, diced
2 Tbs. brown sugar
2 tsp. Amaretto
⅛ tsp. almond extract
¼ cup sliced almonds

1½ lb. Loaf
1 cup milk
1½ eggs
2½ Tbs. butter
¼ cup sugar
1 Tbs. cinnamon
¾ tsp. salt
3 cups bread flour
2½ tsp. yeast

Filling
⅔ cup peaches, diced
3 Tbs. brown sugar
1 Tbs. Amaretto
⅛ tsp. almond extract
⅓ cup sliced almonds

1. Mix all the filling ingredients together and set aside.
2. Bake the loaf according to manufacturer's instructions. About ten or fifteen minutes before the rising period is over, stick your fingers into the dough and make a hole big enough to accommodate the filling. *Do not* use a knife for this, or you will rupture the gluten. Carefully spoon the filling in the hole. Leave to finish rising and baking. Cool on a rack.

SOURDOUGH BREADS

SOURDOUGH BREAD

I absolutely love a good piece of sourdough bread, and this bread-machine version is as good as the best. It produces a deeply flavored, sour bread that rises delightfully high and contains a soft, fluffy crumb.

1 lb. Loaf
 ¾ **cup sour starter (see page 14)**
 ⅓ **cup milk**
1½ **Tbs. butter**
 2 **Tbs. sugar**
 2 **tsp. salt**
 2 **cups bread flour**
 1 **tsp. yeast**

1½ lb. Loaf
 1 **cup sour starter (see page 14)**
 ⅔ **cup milk**
 2 **Tbs. butter**
2½ **Tbs. sugar**
 1 **Tbs. salt**
 3 **cups bread flour**
1½ **tsp. yeast**

Bake according to manufacturer's instructions.

WHOLE-WHEAT SOURDOUGH BREAD

Whole-wheat sourdough is a terrific variation on the regular loaf. The full-flavored grain mixes nicely with the sour, yielding an intense, compact bread.

1 lb. Loaf
 ¾ cup sour starter (see page 14)
 ¼ cup milk
1½ Tbs. butter
 2 Tbs. molasses
 2 tsp. salt
 1 cup whole-wheat flour
 1 cup bread flour
 2 Tbs. nonfat dry milk powder
 1 tsp. yeast

1½ lb. Loaf
 1 cup sour starter (see page 14)
 ½ cup milk
 2 Tbs. butter
 3 Tbs. molasses
 1 Tbs. salt
1½ cups whole-wheat flour
1½ cups bread flour
 3 Tbs. nonfat dry milk powder
1½ tsp. yeast

Bake according to manufacturer's instructions.

SOURDOUGH RYE BREAD

This is my favorite of all the sourdoughs because of its dark, musky flavor and chewy texture. A great choice for ham sandwiches, or to serve with full-flavored cheeses.

1 lb. Loaf
¾ cup sour starter (see page 14)
⅓ cup water
1½ Tbs. vegetable oil
1 Tbs. molasses
1 Tbs. caraway seeds
1 tsp. fennel seeds
2 tsp. salt
¾ cup rye flour
1¼ cups bread flour
1 tsp. yeast

1½ lb. Loaf
1 cup sour starter (see page 14)
⅔ cup water
2 Tbs. vegetable oil
1½ Tbs. molasses
1⅓ Tbs. caraway seeds
2 tsp. fennel seeds
1 Tbs. salt
1 cup rye flour
2 cups bread flour
1½ tsp. yeast

Bake according to manufacturer's instructions.

MIXED-GRAIN SOURDOUGH BREAD

A very dense, gritty sour bread that takes superbly to a sweet spread like orange butter. For a lighter bread, add the optional gluten.

1 lb. Loaf
- ¾ cup sour starter (see page 14)
- ¼ cup water
- 1½ Tbs. butter
- 2 Tbs. molasses
- 2 tsp. salt
- ¼ cup wheat germ
- ¼ cup whole-wheat flour
- ¼ cup barley flour
- ¼ cup cornmeal
- 1 cup bread flour
- 2 Tbs. nonfat dry milk powder
- 2 tsp. gluten (optional)
- 1 tsp. yeast

1½ lb. Loaf
- 1 cup sour starter (see page 14)
- ½ cup water
- 2 Tbs. butter
- 3 Tbs. molasses
- 1 Tbs. salt
- ⅓ cup wheat germ
- ⅓ cup whole-wheat flour
- ⅓ cup barley flour
- ⅓ cup cornmeal
- 1⅔ cups bread flour
- 3 Tbs. nonfat dry milk powder
- 1 Tbs. gluten (optional)
- 1½ tsp. yeast

Bake according to manufacturer's instructions.

SOURDOUGH RAISIN BREAD

This is an especially nice version of sourdough because the sweet raisins play off wonderfully against the sour. Another breakfast winner.

1 lb. Loaf
- ¾ cup sour starter (see page 14)
- ¼ cup milk
- 1½ Tbs. butter
- 2 Tbs. honey
- 2 tsp. salt
- 2 cups bread flour
- 1 tsp. yeast
- ½ cup raisins

1½ lb. Loaf
- 1 cup sour starter (see page 14)
- ½ cup milk
- 2 Tbs. butter
- 3 Tbs. honey
- 1 Tbs. salt
- 3 cups bread flour
- 1½ tsp. yeast
- ⅔ cup raisins

Bake according to manufacturer's instructions, adding the raisins during the raisin-bread cycle, or five minutes before the final kneading is finished.

SOURCES LIST

For best quality and hard-to-find flours and grains:

Arrowhead Mills
P.O. Box 866
Hereford, TX 79045
(713) 364-0730

Brumwell Flour Mill
South Amana, IA 52333
(319) 622-3455

For excellent dried fruit, nuts, syrups and jams:

American Spoon Foods
411 East Lake Street
Petoskey, MI 49770
(616) 347-9030

For an extensive line of gourmet food products and baking equipment:

Dean & DeLuca
560 Broadway
New York, NY 10012
(212) 431-1691

Williams-Sonoma
P.O. Box 7456
San Francisco, CA 94120-7456
(415) 421-4242

Cooking Up a Storm
with the Berkley Publishing Group

REGIONAL COOKING
FROM
AROUND THE GLOBE

__JAPANESE COOKING FOR THE AMERICAN
TABLE by Susan Fuller Slack 1-55788-237-1/$14.00

__CALIFORNIA FLAVORS
by Mable and Gar Hoffman 1-55788-059-X/$14.95

__GERMAN COOKING
by Marianna Olszewska Heberle 1-55788-251-7/$15.00

__MEXICAN COOKERY
by Barbara Hansen 0-89586-589-0/$14.95

__ORIGINAL THAI COOKBOOK
by Jennifer Brennan 0-399-51099-8/$13.00

__THE PHILIPPINE COOKBOOK
by Reynaldo Alejandro 0-399-51144-X/$13.95

All books available in Trade Paperback